To C

MW01146907

THE MOMENT OF TRUTH!

Thank you
Queen !

WAHIDA CLARK
PRESENTS
INNOVATIVE PUBLISHING

BY
ALAH ADAMS

Wahida Clark Presents Innovative Publishing
60 Evergreen Place Suite 904
East Orange, NJ 07018
1-866-910-6920

www.wclarkpublishing.com

Email: info@wclarkpublishing.com

Copyright 2021 © by Alah Adams
The Moment of Truth

ISBN 13-digit 978-1-954161-27-6 (Paperback)

ISBN 13-digit 978-1-954161-28-3 (E-book)

Library of Congress Catalog Number: 2021904281

1. clubhouse 2. Coronavirus Pandemic 3. Productivity Journals 4. Quarantine 5. Daily Planners 6. Work from Home 7. Zoom 8. Social Media 9. Social Media Influencers

Creative Consultan $weet & Tasy Visual Arts
nuanceart@acreativenuance.com
Cover Design by Nigel Walkes

Printed in United States

ACKNOWLEDGEMENTS

This page is always the hardest for me because I have so much to be thankful for, and so many people that I would like to thank and acknowledge. The obvious is to thank the ONE, it goes by many names, ALLAH, YEWAH, GOD, JESUS, BUDDHA, etc. In this work I created a concept to refer to the creator as the ONE. I can't give away the reason why I refer to the creator as the ONE, you will have to read this work till the very end to understand why.

Now that I got that out of the way, I want to do something different. I am going to dedicate this book to one person, my mother, Brenda Sue Adams. My mother was a kind and gentle soul. She was very friendly to strangers and just about anybody she knew. I'm the same way with people, some say I'm too friendly. There is always a method to the madness, so I know why I'm this way, it's because of my mother.

My mother was the epidemy of a great mother! She dedicated her whole existence to her family. She gave birth to 3 children, me, my sister Kiesha, and my brother Carl. We never went without. We didn't always have the best, but we had. That was most important. She was a strong woman because she overcame many adversities in her life.

Although she died in 2019 at the age of 64, her spirit

lives on in our hearts, and our mind. She passed while I was writing this book. Much of this work is inspired by her. I feel closer to her now that she is gone. It's like when she was alive, I knew she was there, now I feel her here in my soul. She is with me always. I love and miss you Mommy.

R.I.P.

Brenda Sue Adams

Sunrise: July 29, 1952 - Sunset: Oct 18, 2019

You will never be forgotten!

Table of Contents

INTRODUCTION

EACE! That's all I ever wanted was PEACE! Finding it was an uphill battle, because first of all I didn't know where to look. It took me all of 44 years to know where to look. I'm here to tell anyone that will listen, look inside for every answer! Anytime you're searching for an answer or the truth, all the answers are right in front of you. Have you found yourself? That is the first step.

I'm trying to stay away from cliché sayings, so you'll hear some things that may sound uncanny, nevertheless true! What is the truth? Is it true just because you think it is? Maybe? I've learned that the only absolute truth is in the moment! Everything else is an illusion!

My goal with this book is to create a road map to your inner SELF, to the core of your being where your greatness lies. To achieve this goal, I believe that we need what I like to call Spiritual Motivation, SPIMO (spee-mo) for short. I don't want to motivate you to make money or fall in love, I want to motivate you to be spiritual. I want us all to really understand that we all share the same spirit of life. When we become spiritually motivated, we want to love and embrace the whole of humanity, destroying the possibility of evil and negativity from our world.

I would like for you to imagine this book as a journey

we're taking together. There will be two major stops along the way. The first stop will be the *moment*, and the second stop will be the *truth*. In order for this journey to be a success, I'll need your full attention and cooperation. Also, I'll need your full trust in my ability to guide you. At the end of this journey we'll both accomplish peace, love, and happiness! And most of all we'll experience the *moment* and the *truth*, which is the apex of living in this existence.

What makes me the authority on the truth? Who am I? Why should you take advice from me concerning the truth? I gained Knowledge of Self when I was 12 years old. Since then my candle has been lit. I'm a published author of 6 books, but there was a book that I ghostwrote that sparked the idea to write a spiritual/motivational book. The book was a guide to love & romance that got deeper into a spiritual conversation. At one point, the team of my client suggested that I scale it down because my client wasn't known to be conscious or deep. When I was ghostwriting the book, I noticed how organic it was to flow with a spiritual concept.

Many shall come, but only few are chosen. The chosen one is the one that chose him or herself. I made me the authority on the truth! Because I have honestly put in the tedious research and reference work and found eureka. I am love in a human form, my intentions are sincere and from the heart. That being said, I urge you to at least give me the benefit of the doubt. You may find yourself, which is ultimately love, and also the truth!

What I really want to provide for you is that moment of

truth! Which can only exist in the moment. We'll discover some things about ourselves that will create positive change, growth and development. It may cause some pain, but all breakthroughs require some destruction in order to build on a proper foundation. That proper foundation is love!

Without further ado, let's get started with the work of finding you first. Then we'll start the journey towards The Moment of Truth! Are you ready?

LET'S GO!

PART I
THE MOMENT.

CHAPTER 1
WHO ARE YOU?

CONSCIOUS ENERGY

Who are you? This is a general question that requires thought before you answer. Most of us think that we are just the person on our birth certificate. It'll go something like this. "Hi, my name is Alah Molek Adams, born on February 3, 1973 in Bluefield, West Virginia. My parents' names are Brenda and Carl Adams. I moved to Long Island, New York when I was 12. I went to Reed Junior High School where I played football, blah, blah, blah!

Newsflash! That's not who I am!

Who I really am is a conscious being formed out of love for the purpose of love. Love becomes the foundation or the purpose for all things to exist. Thus, the term 'make love' which are the perfect words to describe what happens when a man and a woman conjoin to create a being. Even if the man and woman are not deeply in love, there has to be a high vibration of conscious energy in order for sex to occur.

What do I mean when I say *conscious energy*? Conscious is to be aware and to fully know and understand your connection with the energy that makes you a living, breathing being. It is the breath of the spirit of life that is fueling this divine energy. BREATHE! To be living is an energy-based occurrence. All energy has to have a source, ours is as simple as the air we breathe.

Notice how a fire can't ignite without a spark and air. Air fuels the fire, the same way that breathing in the air keeps the divine energy from extinguishing. The minute you stop breathing the divine energy will escape the body to be at one with its source, which is air. The divine energy doesn't cease to exist, only the body dies.

We are made up of atoms, which are particles of light which takes energy to exist. Every atomic particle is conscious or aware of its own existence or energy. Every single cell in your body/universe is aware or conscious of its function or duty. There are billions of cells that are inhabitants in your body/universe. The cells that are responsible for growing toenails can't fathom the distance to the head. In this aspect the body becomes just as infinite as the universe, and the body is the entire universe from the cell's perspective.

There are millions of cells that only work for the moisture in your eyes. Millions in charge of hearing, millions in charge of taste, smell and sight. They are working for the glory of you, the conscious being. To the cells in your body, you are God of the universe. To the cells you are in control of their existence. You determine if they will die out because your habits are putting them at dis-ease causing disease. If you rule your body/universe as a tyrant, the inhabitants will overthrow you. They're willing to die in the pursuit of surviving.

For example, people that smoke cancer sticks commonly known as cigarettes. The cells in the lungs are under attack from every inhale of smoke. The lungs are the home and workplace of the cells that dwell there. The constant smoke is causing them dis-ease so they leave their home in search of a better area that isn't bombarded by poison.

Millions of these lung cells travel to a remote part of the body/universe. The only issue with that is they can't perform their duty correctly outside of the lung's environment. Their duty is to maintain the function of the lungs, so outside of that they have no purpose. They're literally like a fish out of water. The lung cells group up by the armpit and become a mass. Because the lung cells aren't designed to exist by the armpit, it creates a problem in the body/universe. Pain and discomfort become constant, to the point that you need an examination. That's when you learn the mass is cancerous and must be eradicated or the whole body/universe is in danger of death. A conscious decision to end the destruction will assist in rebuilding the body/universe.

On the other hand, let's take a person that is health conscious and not a tyrant destroying their body/universe. This person is a vegan that exercises and meditates regularly. It has been medically proven that a plant-based diet is the healthiest diet for us. No ingesting of anything poison, and only positive thoughts and actions. The cells in this body rejoice and work optimally to maintain the positive vibration created from its ruler, you.

THE ONE

We are all conscious energy. What makes you a living breathing being is the conscious energy of the One, which we all stem from. Therefore, we are all one since we all came from the same source, and we will all return to the source from which we came.

It's like water. The waters that lay in the Pacific, Atlantic and Indian oceans are not different because they all exist in different parts of the world. The characteristics of water is the same. If you put it all back together it will present itself as *one* body of water.

The One goes by many names, God, Allah, Jehovah, Elohim, Buddha etc. Throughout history and many cultures, there is always the concept of a Creator. Because of language there are always different words to describe the same entity. Nevertheless, the concept is always the same that there is an almighty omnipotent being that created everything.

From this One came many. We are all just spawns from the One. If you were able to do a massive DNA test it would reveal that all the blood is linked back to the same origin. We are all related by the same two parents, and they are counterparts of the One. So, it is safe for me to say, we are all one; the illusion is that we are all different!

"Wait a minute, Alah! What do you mean we are all one? It's no illusion, I am different from you. I am a White man, and you're a Black man, if that isn't different than I don't know what is! You're crazy and I totally disagree with you!"

I assure you that I'm far from crazy! What we see when we look at people is a body. That body is just a vehicle transporting the conscious energy of the One. The conscious energy of the One is colorless; and it has no form. It exists in a realm that is infinite, while the body is finite. The conscious energy of the One transcends all time and space, simultaneously existing within the physical realm.

To give you a prime example, a car can't function without a driver. When you get behind the driving wheel you are in control of everything the car does. If the car accelerates it's because you pressed the gas pedal. When it slows down it's because you pressed the brakes. You become the conscious energy of the vehicle.

This is the same when understanding the relationship between you and the One. Your physical body is a vehicle transporting the conscious energy of the One. The One is the driver, the guide, and is always in control of the vehicle called the body. We don't see the truth because we were all disconnected from it and given a watered-down version that doesn't allow complete understanding. Therefore, you'll never experience the moment of truth that life provides. The truth reveals itself, it's just that the masses can't see it.

They have been deceived into believing that we are insignificant and have no true power. They are taught to look for God in the sky and in uniquely named buildings. The truth is that God exists within the body. The only way to feel the presence of the One is when you become conscious of its true nature and existence. Then and only then will you become one with the truth.

Now ask yourself; who am I? I can bet that you have a different answer now than the one you probably had in the beginning of this chapter. When we become enlightened to the truth, we can make a positive change or an extreme shift in consciousness in a split second. It doesn't take years, months, days or even hours. With the right thought process, we can awaken that conscious energy and align ourselves with the One instantly.

It is important that we have a clear understanding of who we are in order to move forward in a spiritual journey like this one. The ego will block your understanding when you have a false perception of who you think you are. Most people can't fathom the fact that we are all one.

Illusions and false teachings cloud our vision so much that we become blind. It's a mental blindness not a physical one. However, a mental blindness is far worse than being physically blind. Mentally blind people can't see the most important things in life. They can't connect with the entire human family to understand the oneness of it all. Therefore, they walk through life never experiencing the beauty that oneness provides.

Now, I want to ask you a question. Before reading chapter one, did you already know a little something about what you read? If not, did you learn something you didn't know that you can agree with? Either way, what I want to show you is that by the mere act of reading truth, we have created a moment. A moment in time! A moment where the truth was revealed. And in that moment, you understood and were given clarity on who you really are.

That's what this book is all about. We're going to keep creating *the moment*. Understanding that from moment to moment we live in the truth because all we have is the moment! The past is gone and the future didn't get here yet. All we have is the moment!

CHAPTER 2
THE WORLD IS A STAGE!

Only ONE actor!

I was told a riddle years ago. It went like this; the world is a stage and we are all just playing a part in an elaborate play, but there is only *one* actor. It took me years to understand this riddle, but once I got it, it became The Moment of Truth.

Now that we know who we really are, this riddle reveals itself. Remember in chapter one I spoke about our bodies being the vehicle transporting the conscious energy of the One? Well the One is the only actor which is playing the part in everyone that exists! The One is always in character and deserves an Oscar for its stellar performance. At the end of this play called life, the One takes a bow and exits stage left. The show is over, well at least this part of the play is.

I learned this concept from being a devotee of Siddha Yoga. While I was incarcerated, I was introduced to Siddha Yoga three times. The third time it came across my path I said, "Let me at least look into it to see why this knowledge keeps coming into my life."

Upon studying the Siddha lessons, I immediately understood the connection. Because I was introduced to

Knowledge of Self at 12, I was open to different forms of powerful knowledge. Siddha Yoga actually taught me the science of not forcing your will on life, let your spirit be the guide. Like a plane being on autopilot, let your spirit guide you through life. When we try to control or force our way through life, we disrupt the natural flow.

This was one of many profound lessons I learned in Siddha Yoga. The one that stood out was about the One or the self being the only actor on the stage of life. I contemplated this knowledge for years adding on to its deep message with every thought. I started out with a base understanding of what the Guru was teaching. Eventually I came to a greater understanding of this profound mantra.

A few years ago, I was introduced to acting. This was the platform I needed to exercise my new understanding of what the Guru taught me. I immediately fell in love with the art of acting because it allowed me to make sense out of this life on a whole other level. I had an epiphany or a moment of truth while listening to this acting coach. In that moment she made the connection I needed to understand the mantra on its highest plateau!

We are all thespians that should be granted awards for our extraordinary skills at acting. We all play a myriad of roles based on the supporting cast of the moment. When you are around Mother and Father, you swiftly slip into the role of son or daughter. As soon as you get around your friends you consciously go right into the friend character. Then there are your kids you have to tend to so you go from the friend character to Mommy or Daddy. At the end of the day you have one last character to play and for me it's the part of loving boyfriend.

You've played several different roles where you had to seamlessly change character. You did it better than your favorite actor in his best movie. And you do this every day! Give yourselves a big round of applause! You all really deserve it for being outstanding individuals! One more time for you!

This is the truth about the One or whatever word you use to describe this undeniable force. Understanding what It is, becomes the answer to understanding who you are. The One is the actor playing the part of you, who is really the One? Does that make sense to you? It is a bit perplexing when you first think about it. You are you, but you are also the One. Kind of like Clark Kent who is really Superman.

On a serious note, it's amazing how the One works in our life. I don't want to sound religious when I'm speaking about the One. This is not a religious work nor is it promoting the idea of one. I'm merely just being a messenger, teaching what I've found to be true through spirituality and motivation. I keep using the word *one* for a purpose that I'll reveal at the end of this work. I felt like I had to throw that out there because I was sounding too preachy to myself.

We act our way through this play called life, most often not coming to great moments of truth. There are those of us that enjoy the beat of life and dance to the tune of the truth. We love every moment of truth life sends our way. Reveling in the blissful essence the truth provides. It's an amazing feeling that can't be described easily with words. When you experience it, you know what it is.

IT IS BY DESIGN!

The masses have a hard time connecting with this truth because it's designed that way. There will always be a group that is dissatisfied with peace, so they will do everything in their power to disrupt it. It is by the design of the Elite1% that the masses are not taught the truth of their existence. It is easier for them to rule a subject that isn't conscious or aware of their own self. The people become sheeple, easily led in any direction.

The Elite1%'s goal is to deny you of any light, which represents the truth. And to keep you in the darkness which represents falsehoods and lies. Especially when it comes to the truth of who and what you really are. They must always keep you in the dark about that because that's how they maintain control and power. At the end of this book you'll find out why it's all about you.

For now, consider yourself chosen. Why? Because you chose yourself. If you're reading this and you connect with these profound messages, it's because the One has become awake inside you. Your candle is lit. If it wasn't, it is now! Everything happens for a reason; nothing happens by coincidence or chance. If you're reading this it's because it was meant for you to read it. You needed to absorb this truth for a purpose. It will all reveal itself in due time.

The interesting thing about the lighting of the inner candle is that once it's lit it cannot be extinguished. This is why the Elite1% works hard to keep the masses' candles from being lit. This would mean that the people have awaken and restored the balance from chaos to order, instead of the current path we're on.

The only way the Elite1% can rule is through constantly creating chaos and catastrophes in order to show the people the reason why they have to always be in control. They control through fear. To the point that the masses will beg to be controlled just for a glimpse of normalcy. But isn't that what the Elite1%, the dark forces, and evil are supposed to do?

Everything that happens is supposed to happen, it's all part of the play. Even when the Elite1% or evil doers think they're successful in their undertakings it isn't the case. There will always be that negative element. What's a good play or movie without some action, deceit, and double-crossing, no good, lying ass people? Answer: a boring ass play or movie. And we can all attest that this play called life is far from boring.

I was taught as an author that a story isn't a good story without conflict. That also applies to the play of life. Even the negative things that the Elite1% does is part of this real life, real time play. The plot thickens as the story unfolds. And it is all by design.

It's always a great time to be alive because the play of life will never get boring. The One will always recreate and redesign the script. As an author myself, my greatest work was always unpredictable. It will always catch you off guard and that's the key to writing a great story.

The One is the best writer of all times! And the best

actor to ever grace the stage of life! The One is playing both parts, the good and the evil, while writing and rewriting the script. And every scene, every act is meticulously calculated to perfection.

The One has many magical talents that we witness in the everyday life. It always comes back to those moments when we actually experience the truth of our existence. Why are we here? What is our purpose? It always starts with love, a real unconditional love for everything living. Then in that moment it all starts to make sense. Doesn't it?

CHAPTER 3
THE FUTURE IS AN ILLUSION!

DREAM OF THE FUTURE!

The beauty of living in the moment is you don't really worry about the future or the past because they're both illusive in nature. The future is more of a concept or idea than it is something that is real. You can use experiences from the past to prepare for the future, but *the moment* is the only reality. People can get so wrapped up in what's to come that they aren't living in the present. We should be active and motivated in the present as preparation for the future.

Setting a plan for the future makes the idea real and when it is fulfilled it becomes a moment. However, the future is just a thought or an idea. We have many thoughts; I was thinking about how I'm going to spend my first million that I don't have yet. I actively put businesses together that can make millions. Until I get there the thoughts are just that, thoughts. However, a strong belief in my ability multiplied by energy will equal the completion of the goal. And yes, the completion of the goal will take place on a later date that we'll reluctantly call the future.

Do I believe in dreaming today and years later those

dreams are a reality? Indeed, I do. I've had some daydreams about goals and upon completion of the goal, it felt just like I imagined. Oftentimes, it came out better than I imagined. Again, the dreams became an actual reality in the present, the here and now which is the moment.

I'm a dreamer, and dreams do come true. The mental realm is where dreams take place. When you become in tune with the One you can connect your dreams from the mental realm, to the actual manifestation in the physical realm. In real time! The mental and physical realms run parallel, similar to two highways that are separate but going in the same direction. When you align yourself with the conscious energy of the One, you create an intersection allowing you to connect from the mental highway to the physical one.

When you're able to manifest your dreams in real time, you understand the moment. Therefore, when you plan, you're connecting mental energy with physical energy and manifesting your dreams in real time. There is no past or future there's only the moment.

Yeah, we know we can plan for the future and everything can work out as we planned it. Then there are times that catastrophic events disrupt your plans for the future. You can never predict these events. I've learned to put more focus and energy into the here and now, the moment. It goes back to the saying: The past is gone; the future didn't get here yet. All we have is the moment.

Don't get it twisted, I'm not telling you not to plan and

set goals for the future. By all means, set goals and make grandiose plans that may take a few years to accomplish. Rome wasn't built in a day, neither is any big plan to succeed. Believe in your dreams and work hard to reach the pinnacle of all your many talents. But also consider a few things about my approach and why I'm introducing different ideas like *the future is an illusion.*

REAL TIME ACTION

When you are setting those goals and making those major plans, make sure that you focus most of your energy in the here and now, the moment! From the moment you wake up, until the moment you go to rest. The moves you make in real time that make it happen in this reality, not just the dreaming part. If it were just that easy to dream up the future and it just happened without any action, everyone would be super successful.

What I'm saying isn't rocket science. I'm just looking at motivation from a spiritual point of view. When I say that the future is an illusion, I'm only being literal in a sense that transcends conventional thinking. Of course, you should look at the future as something to look forward to as far as planning and goal setting. For all intents and purposes of this spiritual/motivational work I'm making a point to solidify the moment. In that case the future and past are not as they appear to be. The only absolute truth is in the moment. You'll hear me repeating things because the Guru taught that repetition is good, and I agree.

The traditionalist would argue every point in this book by nature. I intend for conventional, conformist, traditionalist minded people not to agree with any of my philosophies. In fact, that's one of the magical beauties of writing. Even if you oppose my views, you can't cut me off; you have to listen to me rant. You can't argue with the words on the paper. Being a non-conformist, non-traditionalist, and non-conventionalist makes my points stand out and get right to the meat and potatoes of the issue without sounding cliché-ish. I warned you in the introduction that I was going to say some things that'll be uncanny nevertheless true.

We're going to do a lot of thinking outside of the box. Oh, if you think this chapter is a different take just keep reading. Not only are we going to think outside of the box created for us, I'm going to destroy the box! On this journey, we're going to tap into a level of infinite consciousness that will propel you by quantum leaps and bounds! We're getting there, just a little more and you'll get the whole picture I'm painting. I don't want to give it all away too soon.

CHAPTER 4
The PAST and PRESENT are
ONE!

HISTORY REPEATS ITSELF

I know you've heard the saying: History repeats itself. This is generally stated because scenarios, social patterns, fashion, and music seem to find its way right back into the play of life. Did you ever wonder why this is so? It's because the past and the present act as one. I'm going to demonstrate how the past and the present are one and the same and are intertwined into one singular reality.

In the moment each second that passes becomes the past, but we're still in the present moment because of the time and space. The space that you're occupying at the particular time is all relevant to how long the moment lasts. In those moments that you are in a happy space or place, the moments extend and you experience bliss.

The past is so much a part of the present because of the nature of the two. The present is a transition into the past so much so that they seem to overlap or exist in the same space. It's a divine circle because of the way they repeat from past to present and back to the past. This is how history repeats itself.

Therefore, the past is always being manifested in the

present. The past and the present really run parallel, just like the mental and physical realms I mentioned previously. Again, the same laws apply with the past and the present. When you connect with the conscious energy of the One you create the intersection between the two.

REALMS VS. DIMENSIONS

I must point out that the mental and the physical are realms, while the past and the present are dimensions. The difference between a realm and a dimension is that the dimension denotes to the physical reality, while the realm is dealing more so with the mental energy. Dimensions allude to length, width and depth which are physical in nature. The brain has an actual place/space that stores memory files of the past for the mind to process. The mind processes this data and uses it when it's necessary to connect the past with the present. That's why the past is an actual place in the mind, a dimension.

The present, physical reality or the moment, is defined as three dimensional: length, width and depth. Mental realms transcend all time and space and the three dimensions of length, width and depth. There is always a thread that connects the physical dimension to the mental realm, the thread is consciousness. The being that is conscious or aware of the One is able to connect all the dots between the mental, physical, past and present to understand reality on its highest plane.

Because the past is an actual thing, with physical and emotional attachments it becomes a part of reality. Unlike the future which has no real basis beyond thoughts and ideas. Being that the past really happened it creates its own space in the mind. The mind can mentally go right to that space and play back the tape and experience the past in the real time present. Now you see why the past and the present are interchangeable and are one and the same.

THE MIND IS A TIME MACHINE

Close your eyes and think of a time and a place, and instantly you are there. That's how the conscious being is able to use the mind as a virtual time machine and we are able to travel back and forth between dimensions. The past becomes an actual dimension in the framework of the mind. The mind actually stores all events in categorized memory banks similar to the way a computer works. All the conscious being has to do is go to that particular file in the memory bank and instantly they can experience that part of the past. The purpose is to take those experiences from the past file and sync them with the present moment. This practice assists us when trying to understand things that are happening in our present moment.

The reason you can't do this practice with the future is because the future is an illusion. It hasn't taken place yet so there is no real time experience on the mind's memory file. The mind takes things literal, and there are literally no experiences of the so-called future.

However, you can take experiences from the past file to plan for the future while in the present because the past and present are parallel, thus one and the same. The past is like the best supporting actor of the present. Without the past the present has no foundation. The present is stacked on top of the past; that's how they're able to share the same energy, and the past is able to repeat itself in the present. The past and the present are one.

Ask yourself how does this have anything to do with spiritual motivation? This is the moment of truth where I'm saying that the only reality is in the moment. As I explained, the past and present share the same energy so there is no conflict between the two. However, the future is the only illusion that comes into the play of past and present. The future is like the child of the past and the present. The future exists only as a figment of the imagination.

There is always a level of motivation in this work. The whole point of this work is to approach motivation through spirituality. The spiritual aspect is you understanding who and what you really are, then you'll be motivated to do anything!

This part of the book is laying the foundation because I assure you that most of us don't know or understand our true essence and the power we possess. So far, we addressed who you are, the world being a stage, the future as an illusion and the past being the present. I wanted to establish the foundation, then show how the One is playing the part of you. Being that this is The Moment of Truth I wanted to prove that all we have is the moment by showing you how the future is an illusion and the past and the present are one and the same.

Now for the next 5 chapters it's going to get very intense. I'm going to challenge your ability to comprehend the inconceivable. We will discuss the unknown mysteries of the universe and how they relate to your existence. Then you won't just be motivated, you'll be spiritual motivation in a human form!

LET'S GET TO IT!

CHAPTER 5
THE ILLUSION OF TIME!

TIC, TOCK!

Time is the ultimate balance between the past, present and the future. In the physical realm, time is a calculation of each second compiled into minutes and hours that make up days, months and years. Therefore, our perception of time is based on day and night, or the movement of the sun and the moon. So, we created clocks and watches to measure the time of day for punctuality and for timing particular events.

However, in the spiritual realm the perception of time is quite different. In the spiritual realm time isn't measured by the motions of the sun and the moon, so there's no seconds, minutes and hours that turn into days etc... For instance, in the physical world 40 years could seem like a split second in the spiritual realm. I've witnessed men living their whole life like a savage, only to become conscious in a split second. Which proves that spirituality can transcend all time and space as we know it. We can all become spiritually conscious in the blink of an eye.

When you become spiritually in tune you begin to understand the illusion of time. Your mind experiences the truth and knows that the tic tock of the clock is delegated to this realm. You are time! Because, your mind—which is you—is what regulates the perception of what we call time. Not the watch or the clock. The watch and the clock are instruments that hinder the true understanding of what time really is.

In 1772 Benjamin Banneker built the world's first clock. The pocket watch was already in existence, however there was never a clock. Now what is the difference between a clock and a watch? A watch is portable, while a clock is stationary. Mechanical time is based on the movements of the sun and the moon. That's why there are two hands on the clock, the long hand is the sun and the short hand is the moon. The second hand, which calculates every second, was added to both the clock and the watch for extra measure. Question: Does a clock/watch measure time or moments?

A child is born, and right in front of your eyes the child becomes an adult. You were there to witness every stage firsthand, so you know the exact amount of time it took to reach the goal of adulthood. However, something is puzzling you in the back of your mind about the time. You keep having these, "It seems like it was yesterday," thoughts running through your mind when you look at the once child.

You decide to jump in your time machine and visit those moments you created with the child. You run through a vast amount of memories like a movie in fast forward mode then suddenly stop and exit the time machine and immediately you're back in the present moment. You look at this beautiful person and, in your mind, you question your own sanity; "I know I'm not crazy, but doesn't it seem like this child grew up overnight? Like, where did all the time go? Because it seems to have passed by us very fast?"

What if I told you that time is an illusion? At this point you probably wouldn't be surprised because it's not the first illusion I've spoken on. But yes, once again, just like the future, time is made up by man as an instrument of measure and calculation. What if you didn't have a device to measure and calculate time? Would it still exist? Technically, the answer is no. Allow me to explain.

A CLOCK CANNOT MEASURE MOMENTS

Number one; time cannot measure moments! Moments transcend the mind's concept of time as we know it. Because a moment is created from different types of energy, each moment has its own signature vibration. This would cause you to perceive time differently from moment to moment. Your perception of time is relative to the set of circumstances and the exact vibration of the experience.

You ever heard the term, *Time fly's when you're having fun!* This is why the father/mother asks where the time goes so fast. When you're a good parent, your goal is to create as many fun and happy moments for your child as humanly possible. That's where the illusion of time comes into play. The false concept of time conflicts with the actual experience of the reality of the moment. That's when happiness turns into bliss, and you lose track of time.

You've been programmed to think that the device on

your wrist will tell you the time, and in a mechanical sense it does. But can you actually say that in each moment you felt the same in time? When the actual experience was extremely negative did the time go fast or slow? When the experience was extremely pleasant how fast or slow did the time feel in your mind?

In order for you to fully understand and grasp the moment of truth, I need you to perform this exercise. Put your body in a seated position and relax your mind. Now take 10 deep breaths, breathing in through your nostrils and out through your mouth. Next, I want you to enter the time machine in your mind and go back to a negative experience. The negative experience is going to hurt a little, but pain is part of the process. Then, I want you to visit a positive experience, get lost in the beauty of the moment. This too is part of the process. Now, I want you to try to measure each moment in time. Don't cheat! Did you do it? Ok great! Now we may continue.

I did the same exercise with you. I have done it before so I have an advantage. For me, when I went back to the negative experience, I couldn't really measure the time. I just know I felt afraid for my life. In that moment when you think you're about to die, it's like a flash. I have really bad anxiety from experiencing horrible events. I know I have PTSD from being in the streets and in prison. Believe me, it was a warzone. I have the same reaction every time I visit one of my painful memories. The irritation of the wound in my mind is like picking at a healed scab. It starts to leak blood if you pick at it enough. It's very uncomfortable to visit those moments, but we have to do it in order to grow.

Negativity has its purpose in our lives. We learn from the total sum of our experiences. Sometimes the negative experiences have more to teach. I mean, a positive experience is what it is. When everything is all good there's no pressure to take something from it. When it's negative, you're forced to learn from it to avoid experiencing that event all over again.

If you can avoid feeling extreme pain, would you? Of course, you would. That's why negative experiences are necessary to distinguish the difference from right and wrong and how to navigate through this thing called life. So, everything has its purpose, even the bad things that happen in our lives.

Now let's look at the positive experiences in our lives and how they affect us. When you think of a positive memory, a warm feeling runs through your body. You smile at the enjoyment you were experiencing. You can stay in the midst of this blissful moment forever. Time? What's time when you're in a state of pure happiness?

When you visit these positive moments, you leave with a feeling of achievement, a feeling of accomplishing the goal of visiting a delightful past. It's the total opposite when visiting the negative experience. Your body goes numb and there is no pleasant, warm rush surging through your body. You can't wait until the memory is over so you can escape this dreadful moment.

SPIRITUAL VIBRATION VS. SPIRITUAL FREQUENCY

The moral of the previous exercise was to show you that time is like beauty, it's all in the eye of the beholder.

We must spiritually align our internal clock to be set to the right spiritual frequency in order to create the desired spiritual vibration. You always want your spiritual energy to be vibrating on a high frequency. When it is, you'll experience those happy and joyous moments that make life worth living. When your spirit is vibrating on a low frequency you will experience sadness, dis-ease, misery and a myriad of other negative elements.

It is very important to understand that you must frequently (every second, every moment) align yourself. And that is the only time that exists! The moment! That's why you must always be in remembrance of your spiritual vibration and the frequency which regulates how frequently you're experiencing peace or war within self.

Ideally, we all want to experience nothing but happiness while we live in this existence. However, most people have a hard time achieving this goal of continuous bliss. It's because we are not set to the right spiritual frequency creating the precise spiritual vibration. They work hand in hand.

Look at it like your spirit is an AM /FM radio. You have your hand on the tuning knob turning it to find the right frequency so that you can rid yourself of this hideous static. You know, the sound your radio makes when it can't find the right frequency. The sound is actually affecting your vibration, now you're trying desperately to tune into the right frequency to change your vibe.

You finally tune into the right frequency and suddenly the horrible static disappears. The smooth sound of Jazz music soothes your soul and your vibration is aligned creating that peace you were seeking. Your mind and body are at ease, and there is no negative vibe distorting your frequency, no static just happiness and bliss.

When we truly understand that we are spiritual beings that have to be in tune with the right frequency, we experience true harmony within self. Let's look at the concept of time more like a frequency and a vibration. We will experience the truth that time is of the essence and you are the clock. Your soul and your spirit know no concept of time as it has been presented to us. In its nature the spirit is timeless and infinite, so it will never fathom the false concept of time. Time has a beginning and an ending while the spirit does not.

CHAPTER 6
THE ILLUSION OF DEATH!

TRAGIC BUT TRUE!

T he tragedy of death! I'm going to share a tragic moment that occurred today at 7pm on October 18, 2019. My mother, Brenda Sue Smith-Adams went back to the essence. She was my mother; she was my best friend and a real G to the end. I am intoxicated and high from smoking marijuana. I am so hurt and emotionally distraught that I don't even know why I'm trying to write this now. It's because I want to give you a real time moment experience with me in real time.

Death? What is death? Just because you left the physical realm do you cease to exist? Of course not! Energy never ceases to exist it just transfers to a different form of existence. Back to its original form! A purified gas that exists everywhere at once. Therefore, my mother knows the absolute truth about the entire universe. Whatever was a mystery is a complete understanding. Love is always the foundation. Therefore, I know she loves me and wants me to be the best me that I can be.

Though now, I'm feeling the human emotion of loss, I know she wants me to be ok. I'm all over the place today so please pardon me. I'm really serious when I tell you that I'm just writing to give you the truth of my experience. Let me tell you something, this is the first close loss to me. I feel like a part of me just died. I will never be the same. The pieces are all over the floor and I don't even have hands to pick them up. However, I will survive! I feel like I just died; I'm broken, but I'm here!

THREE DAYS LATER

I'm back, a little better, but still emotionally scarred and sore. I know it'll heal, but for now I'm in the beginning stages of recovery. I'm really hurt because of the thought that I won't get to experience her physical presence. However, our mental and spiritual connection seems to be closer to me. I feel like she is with me more now than when she was here. It's like now that she's left the physical realm, I can actually feel her spiritual energy all around me.

Mind you, this is the first time I'm experiencing this type of loss so everything I'm expressing is raw and true. It's the moment in its purest form. As I write this, I feel a kind of responsibility to document this. This event has changed my entire view of life and death. They are so parallel that they cross paths without interrupting the balance. I couldn't have even attempted to write about a topic like this until three days ago. I feel like my mother wants me to do this for us, and essentially for the world.

I just wanted to spend more time, ah that word time. My perception of time has changed since I started writing this work. So, more time is not possible. I hate to be so technical. It's the human part that clouds my thoughts most of the time, or rather all of the time. I say that to say that my perception of time is an illusion. So, there's no measurement beyond the present, the moment. I have to appreciate the moments spent with my beautiful mother.

Ironically, I have to write my mother's obituary because I'm the writer of the family. Before I get to that daunting task, I wanted to write a little more in this book. Let me take the time to tell you about my mother. Brenda Sue Smith was her maiden name, but she was known as Brenda Adams. She was the second of 5 children from Louis David Smith and Margaret Charlotte Smith.

My mother was her father's favorite, she acquired his intellect. She was highly intelligent with a bachelor degree in business administration. She had dreams of being a fashion model when she was younger because everyone was in awe of her beauty. My mother was exotic because of her mix. My grandmother was Native American and Irish, and my grandfather was Black.

She was a kind soul that loved people. I get most of my good character traits from my mother. I learned a lot about my mother before she passed because I moved in with her to assist her with living. I got the chance to bond with her before she passed on, which I appreciate every day. Those are the moments we created that will live forever. I love you and miss you dearly.

TWO WEEKS LATER

I'm back. It took me a minute to gather myself. No one really knows how they'll react to the death of a close loved one. Writing this book at the moment that I'm experiencing my loss is therapeutic as well as enlightening, for you as well. Because by me sharing that moment in my life with you, we experienced it together. Which is by design. I told you in the beginning of this book that we will elevate together on this journey. I'm not the expert on life, or this work. However, I'm well versed enough to give you spiritual motivation in its raw form.

Back to the topic of death and why I don't believe in the concept. For one, we have already established that the conscious energy of the One, spiritual matter, and the soul, is infinite. It has no formal beginning or ending while the body is finite, having a beginning and an ending. It is the life force energy of everything that is living. You are not just a mere human being as you were taught! You are a one of a kind special edition! Death is a misnomer, a spooky tale told to mislead, misinform and control the masses.

The same way they don't want you to know about life, is the same way they don't won't you to understand the truth about death and the transference of energy. The life force energy that makes you a living, breathing being isn't the same principle as a light bulb! It isn't the traditional, conventional form of energy. This divine energy is comprised of the conscious energy of the One and the spiritual matter I spoke of earlier. It cannot be created or destroyed because it is creation itself!

So, the question is: How can you die? Answer that for me! If you understand everything you've read thus far you know it's virtually impossible for you to die. Your life has no partnership with death. The same way that the night sky and the day sky can never co-exist. When one comes the other must leave. The body and the spirit were never meant to be one because they operate on two different planes of existence. The body is made up of matter, which is comprised of atoms and molecules. While the spirit is made up of purified gas that has no color, shape or form. That's why when these silly humans fight and kill over color, which is the base concept of race, I often laugh. Because they know not, nor do they understand what the absolute truth is. It's all by design.

Unravel! That's the goal, to unravel the threads of the lie to get to the absolute truth. You are the seeker; the truth is a treasure chest! Be diligent in your search, don't hesitate and never go against your gut instinct. Your gut lies where your umbilical cord exists, your so-called 'belly button'. You are connected to the universe through that cord. Even though they cut the cord, you are wirelessly connected to the universe similar to Wi-Fi or the Ethernet.

Ether is the key component in your cerebral cortex, which allows us to use our telekinetic abilities thus the concept of the telephone. Also, the concept of the cell phone technology is attributed to the way ether works in our cerebral cortex. We are mystical magical creatures only because they are keeping the truth about who you really are from you. You can communicate without a telephone or any device of any kind. You can move objects with your mind. You can fly as well.

We forgot how to achieve these acts when we all were re-programmed. Like I said, part of this work is unraveling and getting to the root of it all. What we do know is we are born into a physical world and we die in the physical world. The spiritual plane existed before anything physical. It is the breath of life that gave birth to the physical plane. You are essentially a spiritual being trapped inside a physical body. The physical body being material, while the spirit is immaterial. The spirit knows a realm of true reality that exists outside of the material physical body. So, I used the word trapped because the body is like a prison house to the spirit.

TWO DAYS LATER

Something interesting happened today while I was strolling through the mall. A gentleman that I know named Mark asked me how I was doing. I told him I was okay considering that I lost my mother 3 weeks ago. I told him that I don't believe in the traditional concept of death. And he shared the most enlightening story with me, which I told him I was going to share with you in my new book.

Mind you, everything I'm writing is in real time, the moment. It hasn't been 24 hours since Mark told me this story and I'm immediately sharing it with you as part of our growth and development in this work. I'm going to tell you the story in the first person, as if I'm Mark speaking to you directly.

"On September 11th, 2001, I was getting off of the elevator on the 83rd floor of Tower One in the World Trade Center. I was wearing a T-Shirt and jeans that day. When I got off the elevator and the door closed, the first plane hit Tower One on the 87th floor. The heat from the explosion blasted down through the elevator shaft. I was close enough to the door that the intense heat cooked me as if I was in a microwave. I put my hands up to my face and I saved the area that my hands could cover. My arms, hands, neck and any other area of my body that wasn't covered was melted.

"In that moment I thought I was dead. And for a split second a peaceful calm came over me. I thought I was dead and I was okay with it. It wasn't this dreadful experience that you see in the movies. I didn't even feel the pain in that moment. It wasn't until I thought about my parents and loved ones that a jolt of adrenaline surged through my body. I got up and the calm was gone and the pain immediately became excruciating. However, I managed to get to the stairway and I ran 83 flights to safety before Tower One collapsed."

The moral of his experience was that death isn't this painful experience. In fact, I was told that birth and living life is more painful than death. That's why some say they laugh at death and cry at birth. They understand the truth that this world is no cake walk, that the innocent child is going to experience hell here. In some form or another. But death or transference of energy isn't, or shall I say, can't be that terrible considering that it's over in a split second.

My mother suffered a lot of pain, getting her chest cavity sawed in half three times. Her last year alive, she wasn't living. I know she wanted to live to see her grandchildren grow and to experience more love and happiness. Before she left, she kept telling everyone, "I'm tired. I'm just so tired."

She knew that her time was up and she was preparing herself for the transition. I mean, I know it isn't an easy reality to deal with. It is hard to let go of this world because of the mystery of death, and we have an extreme attachment to this physical realm. We can't fathom any truth other than what we're taught which is very misleading when we look at the facts. This becomes a reoccurring theme when dissecting the matrix. Nothing is what it seems, everything that we're taught is questionable to say the least. The yarn of lies just keeps unraveling until you get to the core which is the absolute truth of it all.

I hear a lot of people having a defeatist attitude when it comes to finding the truth. They give up on the search and have that old, 'If you can't beat them, join them!' mantra. Or they'll say, "Alah, you'll never know the real truth. No one knows the real truth." They say that to say, "So why don't you just give it up already and join the rest of us in ignorant bliss!"

I refuse to join the club because that's what the Elite1% wants us to do, give up. Winston Churchill was probably one of the vilest human beings to live on Earth. I say that because when I studied why he went to war with Germany, his logic was evil and didn't make any sense. He thought that the Germans were advancing too fast in technology. If they weren't stopped, they would be more advanced than the rest of the world. The Germans weren't hoarding their technology; they were sharing it with the world. But Winston was able to rile up the troops with his famous speech where he says, "Never give up! Never! Never! Never!" He promoted this conviction knowing that his intentions and motives weren't right.

Well, I have the same conviction as Winston Churchill, but my intentions are righteous and sincere. When I say, "Never give up! Never! Never! Never give up," it is because I want you to experience The Moment of Truth. So, I encourage you to keep seeking truth from the cradle to the grave! Uncover every stone until you find the jewel. Then place that jewel in your crown. You will find what you're looking for because it's the nature of the hunt. The hunter and the prey are somehow one and the same because they both have one objective. Survival! The choice is yours, what will you be? The hunter or the prey.

We all want to survive and live a modest life while here in this existence. Death is a part of a physical reality, not a spiritual one. The powers that be, the Elite1%, seek to murder the spirit of the masses by bombarding them with strong negative vibrations. These vibrations can never destroy the spirit; however, it can become dormant. You can dull your energy and vibration to the point where the spirit can appear to be dead.

The reason the Elite1% seek to keep the masses' spirits and their souls asleep is simple. It is easier to rule and control the masses when their very spirit, soul, and the essence of life is dead. Not dead in the aspect or the concept that we were taught. When something is meant to be vibrant and living, and you cut off the proper energy, it can give the appearance of death. Much like the animal called the possum. The possum can mimic death; however, it is very much alive. How does the possum mimic death? Simple, by not moving and lying still.

That is the same with your spirit. Once you inject enough negative energy into the spirit, it slows down the vibration to the point where there is no movement. A spiritual death is the worse death that a living being can ever experience. It is similar to being buried alive. The sad part about it is that the masses have become the real personification of a zombie! A zombie is a being that has enough life or low vibration to be alive but isn't conscious. A zombie can't think for himself; it can only search for sustenance to try to keep that low vibration from totally extinguishing. Zombies all move in the same direction. Isn't that similar to the way the masses really are? Don't the masses run with whatever they are told by the Elite1%?

"We don't need you to think. We'll do the thinking for you!" said the Elite1% to the zombie.

"Ugggggg!" replied the zombie.

This is the sentiment of the Elite1% when it comes to the masses. It is by design of the Elite1% that the masses are like sheep, easily led in the wrong direction. They must remain mentally and spiritually sleep, which is like death. The moment we all wake up together, we will destroy the matrix immediately! The Elite1% works tirelessly to keep the masses in this state of suspended animation. They know the outcome if they don't. The Elite1% became the hunter and they created the situation where they have to do this diabolical bidding to survive. While the masses are the prey, they don't know they're being preyed upon but they understand the struggle to survive. It is spiritually draining to the masses.

It has become evident to the conscious being that the masses are no different than the zombies on the hit show *The Walking Dead*! At least when you cease to exist in the physical, you instantly become aware of the absolute truth. The only problem is that you can't return from a physical death to tell the living the absolute truth.

I conclude that you have been deceived into believing in a concept that teaches you that you will cease to exist when you exit this physical realm. You are more than what they want you to know or understand. You will never die, or rather cease to exist. You are an immortal being that will always exist in one form or another. Death is an illusion!

This will end the first part of this work. This is a journey where we're experiencing the truth together. When my mother died, this work took a turn or a twist so to speak. That twist has added substance to what The Moment of Truth was meant to be, a work of spiritual motivation. Let's continue to learn and grow together.

PART II
THE TRUTH!

CHAPTER 7
Stay on the Path!

Is it Destiny?

One day I was speaking with a close friend looking at family pictures. She showed me a picture of her father and I was amazed at how much he resembled a 1970s movie star when he was younger. Unfortunately, he lived a life of drug abuse and despair before dying at a very young age. At that moment I had a question for myself. I do that a lot nowadays, ask myself questions. I asked why he didn't become the successful movie star. The path we all take is what determines our destiny. Most often there are signs placed in front of you to guide you to a pathway of a greater calling. However, if you're not conscious, these signs go unnoticed.

We are all destined for greatness. We just need to be reminded of it, that's all. A little pep-talk with the One. If you were never told or taught the truth of self and what you really are, there is a disconnect from your path which is your destiny. The reason most of the world is content with mediocrity is by design. What determines who wins and who doesn't? Why is there only 1% of the world that are considered Elite1%? The answer to all these questions leads back to the same answer, it is by design.

Is your destiny predetermined? Do you have any control of your destiny? I believe that our lives are predetermined to be what it is. We are destined to be and do certain acts in our lives that are totally out of our control. However, when you are in tune spiritually, I know you can control your destiny. It's been proven time and time again that the most successful people took control of their destiny. They made things happen that even they can't explain. Even when unexpected obstacles arise, the winner persists. The winners of life take the bad with the good and keep it moving. They never allow situations to take them off of the path.

My personal definition of destiny is when spirituality and motivation engage for the purpose of completing your desired task or goal. Life is all about setting goals. From birth, the infant watches everyone walking, in its mind the first major goal was created. From that point the infant crawls then reaches the first major goal of walking. Everyone cheers for the infant for making it to that first big milestone. The infant has the same feeling that an adult has when we have won or attained a major goal. The winning spirit is created, and it's boosted with every goal we achieve.

The Winning Spirit

You must have a winning spirit to stay on the path and endure trials and tribulations to achieve the ultimate goals in life. What are the ultimate goals in life? I'm speaking on those great moments where your actions impacted someone or a mass of people. I'm speaking on what forges the greatest people to change the world. The stuff heroes and champions are made of, a winning spirit!

We are all born with it. Some of us were fortunate enough to have adults around us to cultivate that winning spirit. It's all about putting it into perspective when it comes to who keeps the winning spirit. The vibration of our spirit can be manipulated with sound and thought, provoking energy. An example of how sound and thoughts provoke energy is how someone speaks to you. When the tone of voice is pleasant, the thoughts in the speech initiate a positive vibe. This creates a peaceful vibe in your spirit. When the tone is negative, this creates an uneasy spirit. Feeling uneasy or at peace also plays an important role in your thoughts. So, you see, sounds and thoughts have a major part to play in the development and maintenance of the winning spirit.

It is very important that you keep this in mind when creating the right vibe to win in life. Sometimes there are people that mean well, but they don't understand they are counterproductive to enhancing the winning spirit. They think they're assisting or helping a situation but it's really the opposite; they're draining you of your energy. That causes your vibe to be off, or as they say, left of center. It can be a hard thing to do, but you must cut off those that are spiritually counterproductive. Especially if you can't change their negative patterns. It is essential that you are mindful of the type of energy you allow in your circumference.

Our spiritual self knows this to be true. It is our physical self-that's attached to the ever so evasive Ego, which keeps us from knowing the truth that the spiritual self always knew. It is all about connecting with these spiritual forces that creates the precise vibe so that your mind can transcend and shed its physical fetters. Once that's done you can easily achieve any goal you put your mind to. It becomes so easy for some that they can have a phenomenal idea today, and a week later it's manifested in real time. Now that's what you call power!

It is easy for me, or anyone for that matter, to say these profound things. It's another thing to stay on that path without veering. That's a master! Excuse me, I meant a perfected master! One that has perfected the science of life. That is truly the ultimate goal at the end of the day. To be unified as one with mind, body and soul. It has always been the goal of the spirit realm.

THE REALITY GRID

I established that the main objective of the spirit realm is to unify the mind, body and soul. The Elite1% have a counter-goal to do the complete opposite, they desire to divide the True Trinity (mind, body and soul) and everything that is different. White vs. Black, rich vs. poor, old vs. young, gay vs. straight, Christian vs. Muslim, republican vs. democrat etc. These opposing forces create a social paradigm where being unified is inconceivable.

This negative paradigm creates a reality grid upon which the matrix can operate. What is the reality grid? The reality grid is the network of technology put in place to manufacture what the masses perceive as truth and/or reality. Without the reality grid none of these social programs, which are illusions, can exist. They are a figment of the minds of the analysts in a think tank formulating diabolical ideas for the Elite1%. These ideas are filtered through the many media outlets. And just like magic, these ideas become reality.

Everyone is conditioned from kindergarten to be rewarded for following the rules and regurgitating information like a robot. We are indoctrinated from birth to believe what we are taught with no concept of questioning or validating the information. The minute you start questioning you become ostracized. You become outnumbered to the point that even though you're right and the masses are wrong, it doesn't matter.

The reality grid can only exist if the masses believe in the ideas and information that is disseminated through its network. If only a few people believed in the ideas promoted by the reality grid, it would self-destruct. It uses the energy from the minds of people that believe in it as fuel. Without it, the reality grid has no power. Therefore, it would naturally cease to exist.

A quick example of how the masses could defeat the Elite1% is by destroying all means of communicating with modern devices. That includes all TVs, radios, cell phones, computers, touchpads etc. The only means of communicating would be with letters and actually speaking with one another.

The other method would be to take control of all telecommunications and only teach truth and righteousness throughout the land. No one religion can claim dominance over the other. Nature and the organic ways of living will be the only way of life. There will be no disseminating of anything negative with the new reality grid. This network will create a positive utopian-like society. The positive will be the majority, destroying all negativity and causing all to follow.

Call me a dreamer!

SOCIAL ENGINEERING

All of the so-called advanced societies of the world follow the same protocol. America is the prototype for the rest of the world when it comes to social engineering and psychological operations. Truthfully, America is one big social experiment that has gone out of control. The rest of the world has used America as its model, not knowing the full truth of what America really is.

The Elite1% gets the same satisfaction from evil deeds that the rest of us gets from doing something very positive in life. They are the true definition of sociopaths mixed with psychopathic behavior giving birth to a different kind of monster. Only this type of monster could be responsible for the scenarios created in these socially engineered operations to enforce fear.

They also use social engineering to create social programs that reinforce self-defeating ideas and concepts into the minds of the masses. This is why the masses can't fathom the truth about their relation to the universe. This isn't make-believe, there are a group of people that have been creating chaos from an innate urge to destroy. This negative element was created since the beginning.

The masses are the victims of a vicious game, and the

playing field is uneven. The only way to even the odds is for the masses to wake up and become enlightened on a massive scale. Then and only then will the light conquer the darkness in humanity. I make it sound so simple, as if with the stroke of a pen. Just like that reality is altered. However, this is really the case with the policy makers. With the stroke of a pen the laws and policies are made and the policy enforcers, formerly known as police officers, make sure you don't break the policy/law!

So now let's connect all the dots. What does this have to do with spiritual motivation and staying on the path? These programs take you away from the path and prohibit your spiritual growth. As I said a few times in this work, a lot of this mess is by design. The design is for the masses to be kept asleep and ignorant to the knowledge of who and what we really are. The policies ensure that we all follow the rules and intellectually participate in the socially engineered social programs in order to advance in society. It becomes a societal norm for you to do and think like everyone else. Any deviation and you become the outcast.

CHAPTER 8
THE CYBER SOCIETY AGENDA

HUMAN CYBORG PROGRAM

I'll give you a major example of how social engineering works through social programing. Social media is a massive social experiment that was so highly successful that they have mastered the art of social engineering. They trick you into believing that you're signing up to a free website that caters to connecting you with friends and family. The obvious conspiratorial view would be that the CIA uses social media to easily collect intel on suspects. Or that Facebook sells your personal information to advertisers. That's what they want you to know, the base level of everything. It's the red herring, used to throw you off the trail.

The real purpose of social media is to prepare the masses for The Cyber Society Agenda which is a HUMAN CYBORG PROGRAM, where advanced NANO technology and AI (Artificial Intelligence) become integrated into human psyche and ultimately into the body itself. Social media is the introduction for humans to adapt to living their lives in a computer simulated virtual reality.

The first wave of The Cyber Society Agenda was the

creation of the smart phone. The smart phone is really meant to be a cybernetic attachment, and it acts as an extension of the human body, an interphase. This is why you panic when you think you lost your phone. And when you actually lose your smart phone, you feel like you just lost a part of your body.

This is why the architects of The Cyber Society created a certain pattern of speech when designing the technology. They use terms like '4G' and '5G' which stands for fourth and fifth generation smart phone technology. CELL-phone, which is in connection to the cells in your body. Blue-TOOTH, another part of the human body. Everything they do is strategic, so there's no coincidence why they chose certain words to define the technology.

Once the general public accepted their new cybernetic attachment and the jargon, it was time to create a dependency. Pacify the masses with social programs that lull the brain. The creation of challenges, memes, direct messaging, scrolling, trolling, and certain games replaced physical interaction. Once this pattern is repeated for long periods of time, it's like you can't live without your smart phone and the social programing it provides.

In August of 2019 a research company named Rescue Time reported that people spend upwards of four and a half hours a day on their smart phone. That's like a part time job. That's exactly what they want, people to trade humanity for technology. Technology that was designed to rule, control and monitor your life for the benefit of the Elite1%!

It was easy for us to be integrated into The Cyber Society Agenda because it created a comfortable way to have access to the entire universe. I'm in love with the fact that I can have a debate and we can all go to our phones to find out who's right. Doesn't mean that it's the truth, but Google is like the almighty wizard of oz. You can practically find out anything you need to know directly from Google. Your smart phone can tell you your heart rate, how many steps you took today, how many calories you ate, the weather and anything you need cybernetically.

They designed the smart phone to be as helpful as a personal assistant so to speak. This is the reason Apple, which is one of the chief designers of The Cyber Society, created Siri which stands for 'secret' in Swahili. Siri is the official cyber-voice of The Cyber Society's Agenda. To give you a sense of human interaction despite it being AI.

The end goal of The Cyber Society Agenda would be the actual cyber-human where they'll implant highly advanced Bluetooth and Wi-Fi technology into the body. These devices will be fully operational through your brain's neurotransmitters and receptors. The future of The Cyber Society Agenda is a world where you will be able to start your car and control all of your house's electronic functions. Send and receive emails, receive calls and make them, everything your cellular smart phone can do, you will be able to do just by thinking it. Just like Frankenstein, it will be the creation of the cyborg.

Using social media, they can inject any idea directly into the brain's neurotransmitter receptors. From there they can control almost every facet of human emotion and activity. In the end the world will be like mindless robots under the complete control of the Elite1%.

Technological Slavery!

This is all by design of the Elite1%. They know the truth and will never teach it because it threatens their very existence. That being said like always it's very simple, yet complex. Remember this is chess not checkers, so every move they make is so intricate you will not see it until it's too late.

I've already demonstrated how they tricked us into participating in our own demise by accepting the terms of the technology (trick-knowledge) and the social programming. The final move on this chessboard is perpetual slavery using the very technology we've accepted. The end game, or the goal of the Cyber Society Agenda is Technological Slavery. In other words, CHECKMATE!

It's already been set up with the 5G towers that are emitting increased radiofrequency radiation. The reason for this is to be able to connect people to a network via NANO particles inserted into the body. The Corona virus is just a Trojan horse ushering in the vaccine which will contain the NANOBYTES. The vaccine is disguised as experimental, but its really the final product of extensive research into NANO TECHNOLOGY.

They want you to believe that there was a mystery outbreak and they "WARPSPED" a vaccine in less than a year. Clinical trials on humans take up to 3 years minimum. If this be the case, everyone that takes the vaccine is a Guinee pig, or they already have all this planned out. They know exactly what is in the vaccine, but they can't tell you the truth, that the vaccine really contains NANOBYTES that'll change your RNA to be compatible with the new network.

We are heading towards some trying times. The Elite1% have our futures all planned out. It is up to the Citizens to stand up and fight against this tyranny! The only reason they are successful is because we willingly participate without questioning the motive of these scoundrels. I assure you that once you do the research, you will see that the people that are in control do not have our best interest in mind.

CHAPTER 9
POWER!

WHAT IS TRUE POWER?

There are many definitions to the word power. The general definitions for power are according to Oxford dictionary - the ability to do something or act in a particular way, especially as a faculty or quality. To supply (a device) with mechanical or electrical energy. To move or travel with great speed or force. These are just a few definitions you get when you look up the word power. I'm going to share a definition of power that will transform your thoughts in a way that you will become the powerful being the spirit realm intended for you to be!

When I was incarcerated as a youth, I took the time to join certain conscious groups. While attending one of the meetings, the instructor played a video tape of a lecture done by Professor Leonard Jeffries. He was speaking at a public park to what looked like thousands of youth. I was about 18 at the time.

He said: "Before I go, I want you to repeat after me. POWER! Is the ability to define reality, and have others respond to it as if it were their own." He paused, "Don't let anyone take your power from you! Define your reality!"

I'm 46 years old, and those words are as impactful today as they were 28 years ago. I memorized those words and internalized them; they're a part of my psyche. It's a part of my personal constitution, principle and code of elevating. I practically live by those words.

Let's dissect this profound mantra.

The ability to define Reality

As I began to walk with this definition, I totally understood one thing clearly. In order to define reality, you must first be a free and independent thinker. Somewhat of a dreamer, so to speak. The clear and focused mind that thinks outside of the box and explores different possibilities despite its oddities. The One that goes left, although everyone is going right, out of an innate feeling that something isn't right. These are the characteristics of the One that defines truth and reality! And ultimately discovers true power!

The system is set up for you to be complacent in your comfortable little world. It has defined your entire reality for you from birth. It is designed for you to only see what they want you to see, and to never question the authority. Those that question the authority are labeled as outcasts and social miscreants for not following the rules. From there, they are physically, mentally and emotionally abused. Oftentimes, thrown in jail and most times just murdered. For speaking the truth and exposing the system for the bloodsucking leaches and scumbags they really are.

However, just like in the movie *The Matrix*, there is always One that questions the system. In the movie the

One was called Neo. NEO = ONE. Neo is the example of the One that has become conscious and understands that you only become powerful when you learn to define reality. When he came into the realization of himself and his true power, he was able to see the matrix for what it really was. Then he was able to manipulate and control the matrix instead of it controlling him.

This movie documents the awakening of the One that exists inside us all. We are all Neo with the hopes of transforming into the One. All it takes is realizing that everything isn't what it appears to be, and understanding your power. If you don't, someone else, namely the Elite1%, will drain you of your power and use it against you to control and enslave you.

SUSPENDED CONSCIOUSNESS

Nowadays the truth is arbitrary, not in nature, but because the current reality grid produces so many lies that it's impossible for the unconscious mind to discern reality from illusion. This is done purposely in order to keep the masses in a state of suspended consciousness. In that state of suspended consciousness, the masses are only aware of the ideas and information that is disseminated through this artificial reality grid, which is elusive in nature.

It's similar to the lifespan of a caterpillar. A caterpillar inches itself on the ground, crawling through any vile substance in its path. Subject to being stepped on or devoured by any larger predator. Its nature is to one day create a cocoon and transform into a beautifully winged butterfly.

Being in a state of suspended consciousness is like being a caterpillar and making it to the cocoon stage, but never evolving and transforming into the butterfly. In a state of suspended consciousness, you don't even know that you have the ability to evolve into this advanced form of existence. Therefore, you remain in the matrix being fed on for your precious energy. You're feeding the beast that's keeping you blind to the truth of your power. Kind of thought provoking isn't it?

The truth of your existence is kept a Siri (secret) from you for your whole life. So you never become the conscious being in tune with the self and understanding your true power. When you understand your true power, you break out of your cocoon and become the butterfly you were meant to be. Or like in *The Matrix* when Neo discovered his true power and flew around the matrix like a rocket!

When we achieve major goals and significant breakthroughs, it becomes the proverbial breaking out of the cocoon. When we ascend spiritually, we reap the benefits in our physical existence. This includes mentally, emotionally, health wise, and as it pertains to wealth. It all starts with a strong spiritual foundation.

All these things would be easy to achieve if it were not for the great efforts of the Elite1% to keep you in a state of suspended consciousness. They will constantly bombard you with mental folly to keep your attention away from the truth. The truth is all around you, but you are limited to what's in your cocoon. Therefore, you can't experience it, only the things you're programmed to experience which are false illusions.

The good news is, it's all a figment of your imagination. None of it is real, so at any moment you can wake up and cut the cord that's hardwired into your mind. And just like that, you're no longer in a state of suspended consciousness. Now you can utilize the power you were born to use, for the purposes of righteousness. We all know right from wrong? That's a rhetorical question; or is it? In the next chapter I'm going to explore some topics that I hold to be true. These topics aren't your mainstream issues, and you may not agree. But the lesson is to see things not only with your eyes, but with your senses. I have to prepare you for this one. Are you ready?

Ok, here we go!

CHAPTER 10
THE TRUTH HAS BECOME A PARADOX!

THE PARADOX BOX!

The essence, or the true nature of 'The Truth' has been taken out of its original form and has now become paradoxical. Due to the Elite1%'s success rate with the creation of the reality grid and The Cyber Society Agenda, the truth has been placed in its own paradox box. What do I mean by putting these words together that rhyme? I know, it has a Hip-Hop ring to it, allow me to explain.

According to the Oxford Dictionary the word paradox means a statement that seems to be absurd or self-contradictory, but when it is explained and investigated it is true. For example, I say the Earth is flat and it isn't moving. You say, "That's absurd! Everyone knows the Earth is round and it's rotating around the sun."

I explain it and we perform simple tests, then you do your independent investigation and you conclude that I'm right. The Earth is flat, and the evidence supports the facts that the sun and the moon are moving counterclockwise above our heads. I made the absurd statement that seemed to contradict itself, nevertheless the statement is true. That is how a paradox works.

In the realm of the paradox box it works a little different. It would go like this. I say the Earth is flat and isn't moving, you do your research but you still want to believe what you were taught. You can't fathom that the General Board of Education and NASA would collude to indoctrinate you with the globe, spinning ball Earth, since you were an impressionable child. Or that NASA would present photos to the entire world of the Earth and the universe that are fakes. Even when NASA has repeatedly admitted that all the pictures are photo shopped and CGI (Computer Generated Images). Oh yeah, and that they, NASA, employs more artist than astronauts. You won't believe the moon landing was fake, even when Buzz Aldridge admitted in an interview with a seven-year-old girl that they never went to the moon. Even when Zen Garcia proved in court (not once, but twice) that the Earth is indeed not round but flat.

Today the truth has to be unearthed and dug up so deep most people give up at the thought of doing that much work. It has to be investigated with a microscopic lens before it is even considered to be remotely true. And there would still be doubt to the point that truth is often just dismissed as some strange conspiracy. Then it is permanently placed in the paradox box.

The reality grid and The Cyber Society Agenda have deconstructed our ability to use our basic senses to tell us what's true or not. Common sense truths that you can explain from simple observation and contemplation are extinct. The data in the information used to program the masses goes against your common sense, yet the group consensus is to go with the illusion or the lie.

That's why the truth has been placed in the paradox box because when the actual truth is revealed, the masses will not believe it. They will swear on their whole existence that the truth is a lie, even when their very own senses are telling them otherwise. Even upon investigation the masses will still go with the lie. That's why the truth stays in the box.

ALTERNATE TRUTH

The interesting thing about the paradox box is that it creates an alternate truth. The mind has to be satisfied, it won't rest until it knows and understands the truth. The architects know this, so they had to create alternate truths. It isn't a lie per say, it's just a confusing explanation of something that isn't fact.

For example, one day a truth seeker asked a NASA reject some serious questions because there were some things she couldn't figure out. She was curious, and she wanted some expert answers from NASA since they are the authority on the "spinning ball Earth".

"Since the Earth is round, and Australia is located on the bottom, (thus the term the 'Land Down Under') wouldn't they be upside down?" asks the truth seeker.

"Because of the Coriolis effect it doesn't feel like they are on the bottom, but they are," NASA reject responds.

"What is the Coriolis effect?" the truth seeker humbly asks, seeking an honest and truthful answer from this NASA reject posing as the authority on this paradoxical, yet seemingly intellectual, topic.

"The Coriolis effect is a force created because of the Earth's rotations and movements, it causes objects in motion, and oceanic and atmospheric currents to be deflected to the right in the northern hemispheres and to the left in the southern hemisphere."

The truth seeker is so confused. She stands there blinking her eyes and slowly turning her head from side to side as she contemplates this truly absurd explanation. The truth seeker inadvertently speaks what she's thinking. She actually knows all of the information on the "spinning ball Earth", so she tries to make sense out of it all.

"So, because the earth is spinning at 1000 miles per hour, while rotating around the sun at 66,000 miles per hour, and then the sun and all the planets are spiraling through an infinite universe at 500,000 miles per hour. So those movements cause the Coriolis effect which is the explanation to how Australia experiences things right side up, even though they are really upside down on the globe," the truth seeker scratches her head, "Did I get that right?"

"Right you are!" the NASA reject answered with glee.

"I was beginning to think I was losing it there for a moment. If it wasn't for your expert knowledge on the universe I would still be confused."

The NASA reject actually just did what they always do, redirect you with an explanation that's so confusing that you agree to avoid feeling like a total idiot. And because NASA is presented by the media and government agencies as the authority on the matter, the masses never questions the validity of their information.

If One were to do the slightest investigation, they would find so many inconsistencies and holes in everything NASA promotes. From the moon landing (they recently announced that they've lost all of the film) to getting caught faking footage on the space station, with harnesses suspending the astronauts in mid-air giving the appearance of weightlessness. Water bubbles appearing in footage that's supposed to be in outer space, but they're really in a giant pool. These are just a few examples of how they create many paradox boxes.

The masses become so comfortable in their little paradox boxes that they develop this nonchalant attitude as if the actual truth doesn't matter. As if I, or any other truth teller, am insane for thinking anything other than what is in the program. In the paradox box, ignorance is bliss and the absolute truth is a burden. But hey, what do I know? I'm just a guy trying to get a penny for his thoughts.

THE TRUTH IS STRANGER THAN FICTION

The architects that design for the Elite1% know that once they create a narrative and promote it through their colossal media outlets, that narrative is set in stone. It wouldn't matter if actual footage was presented as evidence to prove the existence of a covert effort to deceive the masses. The people would still go along with their programming. At the end of the day it's all about the narrative and how it's spun. Ultimately, he who controls the narrative, controls the reality grid which has become how the masses gauge the truth.

For instance, let's look at Donald Trump. Yes, I'm going to talk about Mr. President Grab-a-Snatch, by his own admission. I'm not a Trump supporter, but there's a few facts about his term that aren't horrific. For one, he has openly used his power to free more people of color from prison than any president. Yes, Trump has politically pardoned more African American people than Obama. He even posthumously pardoned Jack Johnson when Obama refused. Unemployment is at an all-time low, and in the African American community unemployment is the lowest it's ever been.

He tweets too much, but wouldn't you rather deal with someone that lets you know exactly what's on his mind? At least you know what you're getting with Trump. He wears his ego, arrogance and narcissistic personality on his sleeve. Most politicians present themselves as perfect, holier than thou, angelic beings sent to Earth as the world's savior. They wouldn't dare tell the people exactly what's on their mind. They'd only speak in politically correct terms. Which is just a fancy way of not keeping it real and running game on the people.

If you ask me, American politics needed a man like Trump to shake things up a little. The people were getting weary of these fake politicians. Trump may be an asshole, but he came in and did business. He told American corporations they're not getting the big tax break if they don't bring the jobs back to America. We needed a no-nonsense businessman to step in and do business.

I GOTCHA!

I was just controlling the narrative. I don't care about none of those things, although some of them are true. However, my true sentiment about President Trump is that he's a terrible leader! A good leader would never disrespect the handicap or turn one group against another. That's not leadership; that's the actions of a dictator! And we really have to be careful with someone like Trump in office.

My real views are beside the point. What I want to show you is how easily it is to control the narrative. All I would have to do is create enough positive points and promote them to the masses. After a short period of time the masses would sway in whatever direction they were told. The Elite1% can create false narratives, and even when the truth is revealed the masses will still believe in the lies. If the truth contradicts what they promote through social programming, it's not the truth as far as the subjects are concerned.

The same would apply if they mass promote a negative narrative. It wouldn't take long to convince the people into believing something negative, even if it's completely false. It's all based on their objective and intention. Most of the time the Elite1%'s intentions and objectives only serve their interest, not the interest of humanity at large. In fact, they don't care about destroying the Earth in the name of their greedy and evil fetishes mixed with cynical desires.

Truth be told, the world would be an amazing and peaceful utopia if it weren't for the Elite1% and their diabolical nature. This truth has been known years before my arrival, and it will exist years after my departure. I am such a dreamer that I have dreams that I can restore the balance alone. With enough power, I can enlighten the masses to the truth on the same scale of the Elite1%. My grandchildren will live in a world that has supreme balance. No more wars! Free all the political prisoners! No more famine! No more homelessness! No more bringing drugs into the country and poisoning the people! It's really simple yet complex.

But again, what's a world without diabolical, evil, no–good scoundrels creating chaos? The answer is, no world at all. It's meant to be this way by design of the One. Like I said before in this work, the Elite1% thinks that they're creating chaos on their own volition. When really it is the grand design of the One.

Next, we're going to delve deeper into the truth. We're going to dissect it then put it under the mental microscope and make an assessment. Are you excited? I am. This feels like an adventure on a monumental scale. What we find will determine the direction of our travels in this work. May I remind you that we are on this journey together? I am not a perfected master, nor am I a veteran in the field of motivational speaking. What I am is a conscious being that is far along on the path with the ability to guide you. And for those that have been on the path longer than me, I know you can get something out of it as well. A wiseman that knows something, knows that he knows nothing at all. For what you know is like a grain of sand in a vast desert. Knowledge is infinite.

CHAPTER 11
THE DICHOTOMY OF THE TRUTH!

HISTORY VS. HIS-STORY

History or His-Story is said to be told by the victor. That would mean that it wouldn't matter if his story is true or false. Being that he is the winner of a war that lasted over 1000 years and counting, he becomes the authority. Therefore, he gets to write his version of the story. However, the true version of the story exists and is naturally resurfaced by the virtue of balance in the universe.

I have witnessed how the true story has exposed his-story for what it is. It is a testament to how mind control, social engineering, and social programming meet to form the construct for American society. It is a conspiracy of the highest proportions that perplexed me at first, then liberated me after the initial shock.

That's why I understand that if you're not a conscious being, your mind won't be receptive to the true story. Those that haven't become conscious are still attached to the false reality grid so they can't see anything beyond what they are told. Even when the evidence revealing the true story is overwhelming, his-story prevails. Thus, the term, 'Truth out of season bears no fruit'.

You may be asking yourself, what in the world could he be talking about? I'll tell you what I'm talking about. Let's start with Christopher Columbus. They teach that Christopher Columbus discovered America in 1492. Not only didn't he discover America, there's discussions among the truth-seeking community about whether he really existed. That's another book, which I'm not writing at this particular moment.

However, the real importance of that year had nothing to do with Christopher Columbus discovering anything. 1492 was the year that the Roman Catholic Creed defeated the last Moorish stronghold of Alhambra. The land known as Al-Morocco, later known as America, was set up as a beacon of light and hope for the entire world. After a war that lasted over 1,000 years, America was to set a precedent for world peace.

However, the European powers of that time had an idea to undermine the Moorish sovereign ownership of their land. They decided to raise the Moorish children up and give them biblical names like, Paul, Matthew, John, Michael, Jacob, Ezekiel, etc. By changing their names, they were unknowingly transferring their estate over to their European masters.

Then they prohibited them from reading and being taught to read for fear that they would uncover the scheme. Next, they taught them that they weren't Moors but truly Negroes, Black people, and Colored folk that were brought to America from Africa on ships. Not only would they not have any claim to their inheritance, they wouldn't even have claim to human rights. Because one, they are not even from this land; and two, they have no nationality. Both of these points are per their own admittance. Where is Blackland, Negroland, or Coloredland? There is no identity, and no connection to their nationality, nor the national name of their forefathers. Those were the requirements needed to prove your Indigenous status. With them, you were able to move freely and receive the settlement promised.

Now, ask yourself where I got this piece of real American history? Mind you, do not take anything I say on face value. Please do your due diligence and research, use Google on your phone or computer to look up all of the things I'm speaking on. I assure you it's there when you look.

The first clue is when you put the word Al Morocco in the Google search box this is what comes up:

"Therefore it is obvious upon reflection that the copper-colored Native Americans (Al Moroccans/Moors) are the first people formed in the flesh, and are the aboriginal and indigenous people of America (Al Morocco) and, Al Morocco (A-merica) is the heartland of civilization on the planet."

If you notice when speaking of Native Americans, they put Al Moroccans/Moor in quotation marks, then America (Al Morocco). This is done to reiterate the fact that the words Al Morocco and America are interchangeable and are one and the same. Also, the Moors are Al Moroccans which are considered copper colored and, "are the first people formed in the flesh, and are the aboriginal and indigenous people of America (Al Morocco)."

The last statement, "Al Morocco (A-merica) is the heartland of civilization on the planet," is the most intriguing to me. The Oxford dictionary defines heartland as the following, "the central most important part of a country, area or field of activity. The center of support for a belief or movement."

I dug deeper, because the last time I checked, the heartland or the central most part of the planet was Egypt and the Mesopotamian valley, not Al Morocco/America. At least that's what we've been taught in textbooks. What if we've been misdirected? What if all the textbooks are designed to indoctrinate you into accepting this alternate reality as absolute truth? And all the regurgitating scholars and professors are in on it? What if all the members of elite institutions are under oath to keep it a secret?

This digging led me to the second clue. And it answered most of the questions, enough for me to come to a greater conclusion.

The second clue was a quote from Mr. George Washington:

"If we would agree to take the fezzes and turbans off the Moors' heads and remove the sandals from their feet and enforce severe punishments, and to also swear a death oath between ourselves to religiously and faithfully not allow anyone to teach the Moorish children who they really were or who their forefathers were, and only allow the Moorish children to be taught that they were truly Negroes, Black people, and Colored folks, 200 years from today the Moorish people would not know their nationality nor the national name of their forefathers. Also, they would not know from which land or ancestors that they are descended from."

Around the late 1700s when George Washington made this statement, all the copper colored people were referred to as Moors. In the early 1800s there was an extreme shift, the Moors were now referred to as Black, Negro, and Colored. Then the myth that the indigenous people of America/Al Morocco are Indians and not Moors was taught. Next, all they had to do was re-construct history and change the narrative to say that, "the Negroes were brought over on a boat, we slaughtered all the indigenous people and put the remaining few on Indian Reservations sprinkled throughout the land. All the Negroes are considered civiliter mortuus with no claim to Civil Rights."

Oh yeah, the Catholic Church deemed all people branded as Black, Negro, and Colored as civiliter mortuus. The Black's Law dictionary defines Civiliter mortuus as: "Civilly dead; dead in the view of the law. The condition of one who has lost his civil rights and capacities and is accounted dead in law."

This was a way to lawfully make the Moors Catholic property by branding them as Negroes. This was done to take the land that was promised to them, then to add insult to injury, strip them of civil, and ultimately, human rights. This is the real reason why Blacks have no rights in America, because of a draconic law that is archaic. We are still abiding by laws and policies that date back to 1700s.

So, the land once called Al Morocco, now called America, which was once inhabited by the Moors (that now call themselves Blacks, Negroes, and Colored) is now occupied by Europeans who champion themselves as 'Americans' which means copper colored people. If a person isn't copper colored, they are not classified as Americans. Do Europeans look copper colored to you?

The true Americans, which are the so-called Blacks, Negroes, and Colored folks, are treated as second class citizens that have to march around begging for civil rights. They get slaughtered in the streets like an animal with less rights than a dog. They are the most impoverished, uneducated, incarcerated and face the most health risk, both mentally and physically. Kicked around and disgraced, called all types of derogatory words: nigger, coon, porch monkey and a host of others. And this is all done to them on their own land Al Morocco/America, land of the Moors.

Ninety percent of you, I'll say ninety-nine percent, have never heard of this history in your life. By my calculations, you should probably be having a major meltdown right about now.

This my friend is one of those proverbial red pill moments, where you wake up and see the true reality and not a reconstructed fake illusion that you think is the truth. You can always take the blue pill and go back to la-la land and forget about all this truth you've been exposed to. Or you can go deeper and discover a whole new world that is based upon receiving and reciprocating the absolute truth at all times. The choice is yours.

TRUTH VS. LIES

You see, the truth is like oil and the lie is like water. When you mix them, the oil will rise to the top and settle above the water. The same applies to cream. When you put cream in your coffee, the cream always floats to the top and settles right above the coffee. This is the true nature of the truth. It cannot be held down by lies because it has more density, therefore the energy is stronger.

This is why real history like that of the Moors is bound to resurface. Most Americans have never heard of the Moors and their contribution to civilization at large. I went to school in America and not once did I ever hear mentions about the Moorish Empire or the Moorish people in general. I know this was done purposely to suppress the truth.

The true history is constructed out of real events with tangible evidence to support its validity. Therefore, when the truth is challenged by a lie, in the long run the truth will always win. The truth is the undisputed champion, with or without an opponent!

The fact that the truth has to be corroborated with a witness in order to be valid tells us something about the nature of it and how we perceive it. This point is only relevant in the physical realm because the mind can be manipulated to believe in alternate truths as absolute truths. On a spiritual plane or realm, the alternate truth doesn't exist because there is no mind to manipulate so it has no purpose.

Is something true just because you believe it? This is a

generic question that requires a generic answer. No, it isn't true just because you believe it. Your mind is subject to error and can be a bit whimsical, thus the term, 'Make up your mind'. The mind fancies itself with free will and becomes easily led in any direction it is given. When you understand the truth about the nature of the mind, you'll understand how easy it is to control and manipulate it.

Mind control becomes a simple science and can easily be applied on the unsuspecting masses. If you are taught something religiously since birth, your mind will accept those teachings as absolute truth. It will fight off anything that contradicts its programming. It will perpetuate the teachings to the point that the mind becomes an expert in something it deems as absolute truth, when really, it's just an alternate truth. Remember, alternate truths are only remnants of the truth and not the truth itself.

The awakening of the unconscious mind into the conscious realm is the only way to break the fetters and free your mind! Once you become a conscious being, your mind can never be controlled again. It's all about destroying the old program and re-programming your mind to be able to experience the absolute truth. Most people have been brainwashed for so long that they're not able to experience the absolute truth. Your mind has to be conditioned to handle the truth.

The architects know this, so part of their programming is to place counter measures that ensure the subject can't handle the truth. Most subjects have a meltdown when confronted with the truth. Similar to Neo in *The Matrix* the first time he was exposed to the truth he had a meltdown.

His mind wasn't ready to accept the truth, so they had to re-condition his mind to accept the true reality of their existence. Neo was able to rewire his mind because he was already seeking the truth. But for those that are just sheeple, they will die never experiencing the absolute truth. Although, you'll understand the absolute truth in the spirit realm, the true goal of living life in this realm is to know and understand the truth in the physical realm.

However, most people will not even entertain the mere possibility that the government is conspiring against the people. So, they place their full trust in the same government that is secretly preparing them to be a cyborg with no concept of individuality. A robot that is easy to control and does what it's told.

When I speak of government, understand that the government are agents working for the Elite1%. They are puppets and the puppet masters are the Elite1%. All the senators, congressmen, the generals of all armed forces, the president, the United Nations and all of the world powers are under the direct control of the Elite1%.

So, for someone like me, I'm fighting an uphill battle. The same people that I want to save, will try to kill me for disrupting the program. I become the enemy to the program. For its survival, the program has to vilify anyone that is contradicting the system. Like I mentioned, Neo was a truth seeker so he was able to destroy the program in his mind. So, to those that are truth seeking, which is the first step towards destroying the programming, stay on the path and keep seeking.

Trust that innate feeling you get when something doesn't feel right. You've been there before; your senses are telling you that you're missing something. So you begin to look for the answers. Because the programming is based on control through fear and lies, the confusion always sets in and deters you from waking up. The absolute truth becomes the antidote to this terminal cancer the Elite1% has created.

CHAPTER 12
THE TRUTH HURTS

NO PAIN, NO GAIN!

I've always wondered why they say, the truth hurts. Is it because the truth is so heavy on the heart that it causes many people pain to know it? Or could it just be that the truth is just meant to cause pain and misery and that's just the nature of it? I don't subscribe to that last sentence; I'm just delving into this profound mantra that seems to ring true.

Seriously though, I've always thought about that statement, 'the truth hurts' and I've noticed a few things about why the truth hurts. For one, sometimes the truth has to be exposed instead of just presented in the beginning. Whenever someone starts a sentence with, "I'm going to tell you the truth," it's usually because they started off telling a lie. It seems that the truth is the hardest thing to say, and a lie just rolls off your tongue slicker than oil.

It is easier to cope with the lie than it is to face the naked truth. A well-dressed lie has always had the ability to attract more attention than the ugly truth. In a world where they perpetuate lies as true knowledge the side effect is a world filled with confusion. The people have been lied to so much that they do not care about true facts.

Like anything of value, you have to put in the work to

be conscious enough to understand the truth. Similar to bodybuilding, the more you work out the stronger you become. No pain no gain, you have to be willing to do the extensive research and diligent study to elevate your consciousness. It isn't easy to be conscious in a world that isn't and ridicules intellect. When you're outnumbered 10 to 1 you always have to be on your square ready to defend the truth. That's why the most hated person in the room is the person that speaks the truth. Because this world is full of untruths, having verity is like a transgression.

Although it seems that the lie rules, the truth is so powerful that it will never be defeated. The reward for your pertinacity in the truth is greater than the sum of living a life of ignorance. Staying focused on the mission, which is total enlightenment is always the goal. The outside influences will be overwhelming and you may sway, but you won't fall because the truth got you.

The truth is like a vehicle transporting the spirit. The spirit is the driver on the road of life viewing all the other cars as just traffic. Understanding that the vehicle isn't the most important aspect on the highway, it's the precious life inside the vehicle that's most important.

LIVING IN A LYING CULTURE

The truth really hurts when you believe in something only to find out that you were deliberately deceived. In America, our whole culture is based on lying and creating fairytales disguised as the truth. There's even a national day, not a holiday, just a recognized day, where everyone lies then springs the truth on you as a joke. It's called

'April Fool's Day', and it is celebrated in America every year on April 1st.

"Hey, did you hear about the Queen of England?" I asked in a serious tone.

"No, I didn't. What about her?" Your inquisitive mind wants to know.

"She was arrested for child trafficking and crimes against humanity." I answer, again I'm speaking in a serious tone.

"Really? That's crazy." You are shocked to hear this news.

"Got you! April Fool's!" My serious tone turns jovial and I begin to laugh because I skillfully fooled you.

I'll let you in on a little-known secret. January 1st isn't the first day of the New Year. Based on the principle of the seasons fall and spring, the real start of the new year is April 1st. In fall everything in nature tends to die, the leaves die and fall from the trees. And most vegetation dies out in the fall only to *spring* back to life during the season of spring. This is an ancient principle, and the Elite1% knows this and abides by the real cycle of the year.

Happy New Year is really an ancient Pagan holiday celebrated by the Romans called Janus day. The word Janus is where you get the word January. The Pagans had a belief that they could even out their karmic debt by allowing their slaves the opportunity to be the master for a day. That would mean that slaves could beat, molest, and sodomize their masters, which was the normal treatment for Roman slaves.

The Elite1% gets a real kick out of playing tricks on the unsuspecting masses. The entire world is celebrating an ancient pagan ritual on January 1st called Janus Day, disguised as a celebration for the New Year. While the celestial new year is in spring and it is celebrated on April 1st. You ask why they want to hide all the truths from the masses and feed them lies and fairytales? Meanwhile they celebrate all the real celestial days of the universe. It's a matter of Knowledge being the ultimate power over the misinformed, miseducated, and indoctrinated masses.

Since I was a little boy it's been this way. A culture based on lying. I remember being an innocent little boy, trusting and naïve to the culture of lying. I believed my parents and all of the authorities when they taught me things. Like Santa Claus, the Tooth Fairy, and the Easter Bunny to name a few.

The first one that was exposed was Santa Claus, and that was a big one for me because I really loved that big white man. He made me happy and it was the only time I really tried to be good. When I found out that he wasn't real, I was devastated and I cried for a few days. I remember my Uncle Danny trying to explain to me why everyone lied to me about Santa Claus.

"I can't believe there's no Santa Claus!" I said hysterically.

"It's not that there's no Santa Claus, he's just an idea to bring holiday cheer to the children." Uncle Danny explained.

What really hurt me the most about Santa Claus was that he wasn't dead, he never existed! If he died, then my young mind could reason with it. It makes sense, he was old and it was his time, so there's no more Santa Claus. I could've mourned him and taught my kids about him on Christmas. But no, he didn't die of old age, or a reindeer accident, he never existed!

I got over Santa Claus and I thought, "Well at least I still have the Tooth Fairy and the Easter Bunny." Later that same year I found out that there was no Tooth Fairy, no Easter Bunny, and I just learned to get over it and live in the lying culture. I adapted to it and went along with the programming along with everyone else.

As I became conscious, I noticed that's not where the fairytales and lying ended. I found out that about eighty-five percent, or more, of everything I was taught was fictitious. It was the figment of someone, or a group of people's ideas culminated to form reality. For their own interest, which are all self-appointing and not for the whole of humanity.

I began to uncover and discover many lies and fairytales. I was able to quickly make the connection as to why the lie was spun, for who and how it benefited them. I kept digging and with each fact I felt gratification for knowing and exposing the plot. If only to myself, I felt this amazing feeling of accomplishment that only a true philosopher could explain. It becomes self-gratifying like a mental masturbation, that's my carnal mind trying to explain something transcendental. But you get it.

I have a friend and I always try to tell him when I have these epiphany moments. It's so profound I want to share it with my close ones and my relatives. And he would respond the same way, "If it isn't lining my pockets, then how is it benefitting me? I don't want to hear all that history and stuff because it's like you're spinning your tires in the mud with all that stuff."

I had a hard time answering that question, even though I knew the full answer. I had a hard time because I was met with so much negative force. If I were to match his negative energy, we would both try to kill each other. The energy was so intense that I gracefully bowed out of the argument. Hey look, if you believe all the lies, although the inconsistencies are evident, it's on you. I chose to let him drown in his own iniquity instead of going down with a drowning man that can't swim.

That's when I understood why most of the population has that same mentality. It's because the architects designed it that way and they're above the mark of being successful in their undertakings. If I wasn't already conscious when I discovered the truth about the Moors, I would've reacted like all the unconscious people I know. Like it isn't a big deal, if it isn't making me money.

Even though I was conscious when I learned the history of the Moors, I still had questions. Like this can't be true, they had to bring some slaves over on a boat. Why would they go through such great measures to ensure that the truth isn't taught to the masses? At every turn I became more frustrated. A people's whole history has been erased from the annals of time by just perpetuating lies. It perplexes me that it was even done in actuality.

THE TRUTH IS A CURE TO THE PAIN.

I was hurt to learn that the great history of the Moors was erased, and I still feel the pain of not knowing my real heritage and ancestry. You have all these so-called Black people going to Ancestry.com to find out their lineage. Not once do they mention the word Moor, as if that was never a word used to describe the Blacks. They always lead you to some country in Africa, which I know is a sham. Yes, the so-called Black people do come from Africa, we migrated to America thousands of years ago. All one would have to do is Google the Olmec civilization. They left over 17 monolithic colossal stone heads sculpted out of basalt which is volcanic ash. Each one weighing between 6 and 50 tons! Before Europeans founded their first civilizations, we were in Al Morocco/America.

I contemplated on these facts and after some time it brought me a sense of peace and solace. After the pain came gratification, like the sun shining bright after a storm. The truth became medicinal to the pain. I needed to pursue the path that I was on. It became a burning desire, like breathing, I had to continue the search.

One day while I was going over the information, I had an epiphany. It came to me like a flashback in time. When I was incarcerated as a youth, I surrounded myself with elder statesman that were the wisest men in the jail. I recall a profound statement made by one of those wise men. He said, "The truth hurts, but to some, the truth becomes a cure to the pain." Those are my sentiments exactly. I was digging up as much truth as I could, and the more I found the more powerful I became, because learning these truths truly empowered me. The pain began to dissipate, just like those dissolvable stitches that disappear as you heal.

The real answer to my friend's negative statements and notions was that discovering information that was meant to be a secret, because men took oaths to conceal it, was like striking gold. More so, it was the medicine I needed to cure this innate pain I was feeling from not knowing the truth.

I found out this much with just a little digging. Its right in front of your face, but you can't see it. Once you get exposed to it, this insatiable need to know more is born. At least that's what happened to me, so I can't speak for everyone. However, for most of the truth seekers it's the same wonderful feeling of continuing to know and uncover the truth.

WHEN DID THE TRUTH BECOME A CONSPIRACY THEORY?

There's a little mind game that the architects like to play on the masses. I like to call it 'Conspiracy Theory or Truth'. It's similar to 'Truth or Dare', the only difference is that there is no dare. Also note that the architects have rigged the game by making the truth look like it's a conspiracy theory, while at the same time promoting half-truths and fairytale lies as the absolute truth.

The contestant is given a series of statements and asked

to answer if the statement is just a conspiracy theory or if it's the truth. Also, in this game, it's the conscious being/truth seekers against the Elite1% and their architects trying to influence the minds of the masses. The team that influences the most minds is the grand champion and will get to rule over the minds of the masses.

The Elite1% have the colossal media conglomerate, General Board of Education, and all of the powerful organizations of the world on their side. The conscious beings/truth seekers have the absolute truth at their disposal, but they are limited in the platforms to disseminate the absolute truth to the masses. Also, the fact that the Elite1% gets to the masses first, the absolute truth becomes viewed as mere conjecture. Because of these advantages, the Elite1% has been able to influence more minds and are able to control the game for the last 500 years!

For example, I first learned about the flat-Earth from surfing YouTube. There was a suggestion box pointing to other topics I might find interesting. The first time I entertained the idea of a flat-Earth was in 2014. A young man by the name of Eric Dubay was the leading 'Flat Earther' on the planet at the time, and probably still is. He had more videos speaking on and proving the Earth was flat than anyone else at that time. In no time, Eric's YouTube page had almost 1 million subscribers and his videos were going viral. If you ask me Eric Dubay single handedly carried the Flat Earth movement on his back.

This was back in 2014, since then YouTube has been heavily censoring channels like Eric Dubay's that have absolute truth as its primary content. The absolute truth was waking up too many minds creating truth seekers that were challenging the system. YouTube began to take down all of Eric's work and heavily censored all of his new videos on the flat-Earth. When you go on his page, you'll find strange videos of a cartoon that Eric Dubay didn't upload to his channel.

Then they deployed a counter tactic called debunking. With this new debunking tool, the Elite1% were able to derail anyone seeking the truth about the flat-Earth. This was an ingenious tactic because of two things: it allowed the sheeple of the world to feel validated in their fantasy of the spinning ball Earth, as Eric Dubay would call it. And two, it fueled the anti-flat Earth movement where they don't do any research and all of their theories are easily debunk-able.

And when a major victory is made by the flat-Earth community the colossal media conglomerate will not report it to the masses. Like the Globe vs. Flat Earth court case where a Flat Earther named Zen Garcia won in court not once but twice against a Globe Earther named William Thompson. They do not want the masses to know anything that contradicts the lies the Elite1% have been perpetuating.

So you see how the truth is perceived as just another conspiracy theory. And the narrative of lies and deceit are continuously spun. All the organizations are in cahoots and they're all siphoning billions in taxpayer money into a space program that is fake! NASA is as real as a Hollywood movie set.

The newest fake space program is the one that President Trump is introducing called Space Force. Space Force is similar to the space program that President Ronald Reagan introduced in the 1980s called The Strategic Defense Initiative Organization, also known as Star Wars. The final cost of Star Wars was estimated at 400 to 800 billion dollars, which was reported in November of 1984. The estimated cost of President Trump's Space Force is only a mere $2 billion, in comparison to Star Wars, that's a drop in the bucket. However, the United States Space Force is a proposed branch of the United States Armed Forces. It will be organized as a military service branch within the Department of the Air Force.

All of these space programs are just like NASA, a huge hoax! Its primary function is to drain and extort the American people of tax dollars. Then the government lines their pockets with the money collected for a space program that they know is a fraud to begin with.

How is it a conspiracy theory when one has tons of evidence to support a truth? And if you conspire against me how is it a theory? It's a conspiracy and not a conspiracy theory because I have the proof. It's different when it's just conjecture, there's proof so there's no more theory involved. It is to the point that the absolute truth is being held captive, and an imposter exists in his place. The impersonator seems to be the personification of the absolute truth. However, upon close examination the imposter is exposed and the absolute truth will prevail.

For the meantime, the reality and the truth are still under siege. It's going to take a miracle or some type of phenomenon to correct the wrongs of this corrupt society. This go around it looks very bleak for the team I'm sure we all want to win. As it does in every battle fought against the evil doings of the Elite1%. This is a very old war; it has just been a cold one for the last 500 years. World WAR III is upon us!!!

CHAPTER 13
LOVE IS THE TRUTH! THE TRUTH IS LOVE!

WHAT'S LOVE GOT TO DO WITH IT?

What's Love Got To Do With It' was a hit single from the incomparable Tina Turner. It asks a delicate question that is only pertinent in the physical realm, because on a spiritual plane that wouldn't even be a topic. It's like asking, "Why is water wet?" It's just the nature of the substance we call water. But you wouldn't know what wet was until you came in contact with water itself. It's the same with love, you wouldn't understand love until you experience its true power.

The spiritual plane would view that question and answer it clearly; love is everything! Love has everything to do with life, liberty and the pursuit of happiness. Love is the foundation, the purpose, and the reason for life to exist. It is the fabric of life; you want to wrap yourself up in love and embrace life. You can't describe how it looks or how it smells. It has no color, ethnicity or physical characteristics. Love is the most powerful and uplifting human emotion in the universe, hands down. It is the reason we wake up; it becomes the purpose for living. Love is the cornerstone of life.

Let's take an introspective look at love and how it works in the universe and in our personal lives. Love is essential for the growth and development of a healthy winning spirit. We are made out of love, thus the term, make love. Studies show that infants that don't receive love in the form of coddling and cooing, can die from lack of human affection. It is crucial that love is an integral part of an infant's first stages of living life. Throughout life there is always a need to connect with another human being to experience love.

Do you need another person to experience love? We know we want to feel loved and revered by friends and family. Some get love from millions. In the case of celebrities, millions of fans love a person they barely know. Just from a song or maybe a hit show or a movie; whatever it is, the fans feel a deep connection with these stars. How is that? How can you really love someone you don't know? Is it possible? Obviously, it is because we see the physical manifestation of the love a fan has for their favorite celebrity. The crying, shaking and passing out when in the presence of a star.

Although we see what appears to be genuine love, I think the love a fan has for a celebrity is a bit superficial. Only because I've witnessed the fall of a star and how all of those fans that once loved them, were quick to kick them when they were down.

IT'S A THIN LINE BETWEEN LOVE AND HATE!

Look at Bill Cosby a/k/a America's Favorite Dad. I'm

one of the few that actually studied his case because I was curious. Everyone should know that every court case in America is public information and anyone can view the specifics of any case. It's called The Freedom of Information Act; it is a law and you can't be denied access to court cases.

How did Bill Cosby, America's Favorite Dad become a monster? I mean based on what he was accused of, there should have been signs indicating that this man was a predator. None of the women he worked with accused him of anything, they all said he was the consummate gentleman. However, there were 50 women that came forth to say that he drugged them and then sexually assaulted them.

I did a little digging and I found out that 49 of the women that accused Bill Cosby were dismissed because of discrepancies of the dates and times of the accusations. Only one of the accused, Andrea Constand, actually knew Bill, and they admitted to being in an adult relationship and having consensual sex. So how did two adults having consensual sex turn into Bill Cosby being accused of drugging and sexual assault?

This is a very important question, because something was very peculiar about the way the media reported or the lack of. They never reported to the masses that some of the 49 women admitted that they were accusing Mr. Cosby for the money they were offered to do interviews about him. It was also proven that some of the women were known opportunists that should've never gotten the time of day. But the media still publicly dragged America's Favorite

Dad through the mud. Let the media tell it, Bill Cosby was guilty before the trial started, and that's just what they wanted the public to think.

This was an old fashion public lynching without the tree and the noose. It's obvious upon researching the case that Mr. Cosby pissed off the Elite1% to the point that they wanted to destroy him mentally and financially. What did he do to make the Elite1% want to do this to America's Favorite Dad? Some say he wanted to buy NBC and the Elite1% didn't want a Black man owning a television station. Especially a conscious Black man that was actively teaching the truth of history.

In the end, he was found guilty of three counts of aggravated indecent assault on April 26, 2018. He was sentenced to 3 to 10 years on September 25, 2018. It is 2020 and Bill Cosby is 82 years old. He will have a hard time surviving in that environment at his age. I feel for him because if you read the minutes of the case, Bill Cosby is an innocent man that was falsely accused and publicly destroyed.

Why am I speaking on Bill Cosby in reference to love? It's proof that the thin line between love and hate is very real. But in Bill Cosby's case, I don't call that real love, because all it took was some accusations to get the world to flip. However, if the media machine is so powerful that they can make the world hate America's Favorite Dad, they can effectively promote extreme love in the world as well. I wouldn't hold my breath waiting for that to happen. But hey, I'll say it again, I'm a dreamer.

THAT'S THE WAY LOVE GOES!

When I was a young man, I asked myself a question, why do White people hate Black people so much? Is it really because of our skin? I mean from my view, it should be Black people perpetuating the type of degradation towards Whites for their indelicacies. History tells a frightening tale of the White man that isn't pleasant when it comes to the relationship between White people and Black people. I don't want to go into detail, but we all know that Blacks in America get treated the worst.

As I grew, I accepted this truth about America and I made the best situation I could understanding that fact. I was never one to hate anyone, I've had and still have deep relationships with White people that I love dearly. What I learned about the hate is that you cannot hate something you don't deeply love. Allow me to elaborate, what I discovered about good old love.

You've been in a deep relationship before, right? Did you ever end up hating someone that you once professed your undying love for to the world? Of course you have, we all have. Like the beautiful and talented Janet (Miss Jackson if you're nasty) once said, "That's the way love goes." Was she right or was she right?

That is exactly how love goes. And that's how hate goes too. You can't have one without the other. They kind of co-exist in an uncanny way. They are both two extremes of one thing which is a powerful emotion. On one end, you have the sweet and alluring love which represents all things that are good and righteous. On the other end of the spectrum, you have bitter and disgruntled hate which represents all that is bad and evil. That's why love and hate are interdependent, because you wouldn't know what true love is until you experience its equal opposite, hate. Love and hate are like identical twins, one being the complete angel, while the other is literally a demon. It's the nature of the universe, and *over* standing the balance is what gives us peace.

So in essence what I'm saying is that White people are secretly in love with Black people. They love our ability to create new slang, thus the last few popular words we created were inducted into the American Lexicon. They love the way we sing and dance, our full lips, our women's voluptuous shapes and skin tones. Proof of this is the phenomenon of tanning, lip injections, and butt surgeries that have become the norm among White women.

Let's not forget the mega influence of Hip-Hop on not just American pop culture but world culture. Let's be honest, for the last 30 years Hip-Hop has single-handedly shaped pop culture in America. From fashion, art, to new slang, Hip-Hop has become the ethos of pop culture in the world. Thirty-five years ago, every White kid in America listened to Rock and Roll, today 90% of the die-hard rap fans are White. White rappers are springing up everywhere emulating the culture. It is simply because you love the creators of the Hip-Hop culture, not just the culture itself.

This anomaly goes back to Black face and Elvis Presley. Whites always held other white entertainers up with high esteem if they were able to imitate their Black counterparts well. We live in a country that developed a culture based on hating and degrading Blacks, while secretly loving them at the same time, to the point of imitating Blacks for entertainment. As they say, imitation is the best form of flattery.

You know I'm telling the absolute truth. You know you love us, White people. What would the world be without Black people? Like food with no flavor, or chicken with no skin. You get what I'm saying, the world needs all flavors. So let's open up our hearts and love. Love unconditionally, for no reason. Love every human just for existing. Love every insect, animal and every living thing. You'll experience the truth in that moment: everything is connected and we must love and respect or all is lost.

CHAPTER 14
THE MOMENT WE'VE ALL
BEEN WAITING FOR!

THE CORONAVIRUS!

It took me a bit longer than I anticipated to compete this work. We know that the One moves in mysterious ways, sometimes things happen for a reason that isn't clear at first glance. I know that I'm supposed to make my last chapter in this work about what's going on in the here and now, the current moment. This is The Moment of Truth so I'm going to tell the truth and nothing but the truth so help me One.

As of March 2020, the entire world is on lockdown disguised as a quarantine. The Elite1% have been planning and plotting this event for years, since the first major outbreak of HIV/AIDS. It has been proven that HIV/AIDS is a man-made disease that was used as a weapon to destroy gays and minorities. From HIV/AIDS, we've witnessed the rise of man-made viruses like SARS, H1N1, Ebola, Swine Flu, Bird Flu and the latest coronavirus. They are all being used as an invisible weapon to kill off the population, or as the Elite1% call it, population control.

Hardcore proof that a powerful rogue health

organization exist, was the false 'Swine Flu' pandemic declared by the World Health Organization (WHO) IN 2010. It was a failed attempt because the Mainstream Media still had ethics in journalism. They were able to thwart the WHO'S attempt by simply doing research and holding WHO accountable for inconsistencies.

An article in the Forbes Magazine from May 2010 titled: "Why the WHO faked a pandemic", was mysteriously removed from their website in Oct 2020. Luckily, millions of truths tellers were able to save it and share it, so I was able to find it on a site called; evidencenotfear.com. In the article epidemiologist Wolfgang Wodarg from the Parliamentary Assembly of the Council of Europe (PACE), has declared that the "false pandemic" is "one of the greatest medicine scandals of the century." The article went on to hammer the WHO for trying to change their definition of a pandemic when only 110 people died worldwide.

In fact, the last paragraph of this article reads like a victory statement: "Chan's dream now lies in tatters. All the WHO has done, says PACE's Wodart, is to destroy "much of the credibility that they should have, which is invaluable to us if there's a future scare that might turn out to be a killer on a large scale."

Little did Mr. Wodart know, 10 years later that the WHO would strike back with a vengeance. Ordering the complete lockdown of the entire globe. Ordering that everyone wear a mask and social distance. The WHO would get the last laugh.

For years truth tellers, falsely labeled as conspiracy theorists, have been warning the citizens of America about a sinister plot like this one. Warning the masses of the Elite1%'s evil plan of a One World government that would begin with a mass genocide of some kind. They plan to create chaos on a world scale, then use the staged act to lock down the world. Next, they would declare Marshall Law suspending the Constitution. The last step would be to dissolve the old Constitution and replace it with a new one ushering in what they openly call 'The New World Order'. Conspiracy Theory 101 in a nutshell or absolute truth? For the future of humanity, I despise the answer to this question. Because if they're successful we will have no rights only privileges, and totalitarian rule will be in effect.

Those of us that have been studying the truth behind world events knew this day was coming. We had been ranting about the New World Order and the Illuminati and everything remained calm. On the surface we all looked like lunatics that just escaped the psych ward and needed to be heavily sedated for our conspiracy theories. Because the Elite1%'s moves were incredibly subtle like a farmer fatting up his livestock for the slaughter. Rocking the masses to sleep so they wouldn't see it coming.

That's exactly what they did with this coronavirus. One day we were all free to move about, enjoying what little freedom we had left. Then out of nowhere they announced that there is a pandemic and everything is shut down and we are all ordered to stay in our houses. The mainstream media quickly got to work spreading falsehoods through their propaganda machine saying that the hospitals were overwhelmed with coronavirus cases. The death tolls were skyrocketing and we all needed to stay 6 feet from each other or the virus would spread exponentially wiping out humanity.

Stage one was a success. They were able to fool the public into locking themselves down because of a virus. The lockdown disguised as a quarantine, was an ingenious tactic that got stage one accomplished without using an ounce of force. Then all the media had to do was force feed the narrative that the death tolls are rising and the spread of the disease is reaching critical numbers. The people believed every word without question and it seemed that the Elite1%'s plans were going better than expected. They were ready to celebrate a premature victory because they couldn't foresee what was about to take place.

FOILED AGAIN!

This real life, real time story is unfolding like a Saturday morning cartoon. You have the super villains called the Elite1%, with a diabolical plan to create an air born, super virus to kill off the population. Then they plan to enforce mandatory vaccinations that all the world's governments will be obligated to pay enormous amounts of money to purchase. This will give the Elite1% the power and control they need to make them the totalitarian rulers of the planet.

The masses believe that the Elite1%'s representatives, the mainstream media, are an honest and reputable source of true information. If the information is coming from the mainstream media, it's virtually gospel to the masses of sheeple under the spell of the propaganda machine created by the Elite1%. They have manufactured this enormous feeling of fear and anxiety from the coronavirus hoax.

An increase in fear weakens the immune system and also creates a thought frequency of helplessness and vulnerability. It is crippling society into a nervous frenzy and over time it will create a social disorder that will be irreversible. After a year of this sinister plan the Elite1% will not have to force their control, the masses will beg to be controlled in exchange for some of the basic human normalcies.

I was told a long time ago that fear is the easiest way to control a person. Think about when you were a little kid, the fear of getting an ass whooping kept you in line for the most part. Respect for authority has turned into a game where they plant fear in you through the threat of taking your freedom or your life.

So, in the case of the coronavirus, the fear is very real. People are afraid to contract this "killer disease" that seems to be air born. Everyone run for cover! Corona is coming! Just kidding. But seriously, the amount of fear that the media has promoted has worked like a charm. I've never witnessed this type of fear mongering in my life.

But wait, over there something is rising! Out of the ashes of hopelessness and despair there is a savior, a hero. Not one, but many, wait a minute, in a split second that small number turned into thousands, now millions. It looks like the people are using the internet and social media against the Elite1% and their mainstream media! The masses are resisting the spell cast by the mainstream media and they're becoming informed by a different source of information.

They are calling themselves the citizen journalists and their enemy is the mainstream media. The citizen journalists came up with an ingenious plan to use the internet, which is a component of the propaganda machine, to reverse the polarity of the false information disseminated by the mainstream media. The truth that citizen journalists posted on the internet went viral and millions were able to dispel the myths generated by the mainstream media, wounding their precious coronavirus hoax.

All of a sudden, the mainstream media had to scale down the number of deaths they were falsely reporting daily. The push back from the citizen journalists was so powerful that the Elite1% had to recalibrate the propaganda machine. They created a new algorithm that would inject doubt in any citizen journalists' post on social media. The posts of actual doctors working at Elmhurst Hospital in Queens, New York at ground zero were deleted, because they said the doctors were reporting misinformation.

They created fake citizen journalism groups as a measure to try to control the narrative of the real citizen journalists. It didn't work because for every fake post, one-hundred real posts were being circulated. Then the truth seekers began to repost the real citizen journalists by the thousands. The Elite1% could not stop the flow of post made by the army of real citizen journalists so they were forced to shut it down.

Foiled again! The citizen journalists have saved the day for the whole human family. We need to hold a parade for the many journalists that put their careers and lives on the line to save us all from the plight of the Elite1%. The Elite1% isn't done attempting their evil plan, but for now all is safe. The government has opened back up and things are slowly going back to normal.

TALK ABOUT A CLOSE CALL!

I don't think the masses of sheeple really know what just happened. The whole world was about to be transformed into this apocalyptic version of the *Hunger Games*. The Elite1% just reared their ugly monstrous heads out of the closet showing us what they are capable of. We were all about to be doomed in the worst way. The Elite1% are going to use this as a proverbial litmus test to see how they will attempt this again. Only next time they're going to dismantle the internet, and any platform that shares information rapidly with the masses.

This was also a test for the people. It showed us that at any minute your freedom can be taken. It will remind us all that freedom is a precious commodity. In America where there is an abundance of resources, being unable to get simple things like toilet paper was devastating. Not being able to spend hundreds on eating out and wasting food, or not being able to go to the mall to foolishly spend not hard-earned money. The spoiled little Americans got a glimpse of the hard life. Yeah, I think we could've used a reality check to go with the stimulus check.

I believe that when the smoke clears from this coronavirus hoax, we are all going to be closer despite the social distancing policy. Americans had a taste of what it's like in a third world country where the government can enforce policies with no freedom to protest. Americans are pacified and pampered, so this was the ultimate wakeup call for us. We will not be taking things for granted so much, and I believe we will be a bit kinder to one another. Or at least I hope something good will come out of this fiasco.

One thing's for sure, the Elite1% are not going to stop there. I'm sure they have a few more tricks up their sleeves. But this time we'll be ready; yes, I said we'll be ready because I was one of the citizen journalists that helped to save the day! I was creating live content dedicated to spreading the truth about the coronavirus hoax. I was posting and reposting important information and also speaking with my loved ones about the hoax.

You have to remember, if we don't spread the truth to our loved ones, and they end up victims to this hoax the blood is on our hands. If you're a person that was already actively researching conspiracy theories online, you were already prepped for this work. Those of us that were already hip to the moves of the Elite1% were able to grasp and uncover the hoax for what it really was and quickly share it.

I want to thank all of the courageous citizen journalists, whom I call The Millennial Heroes' that stepped up to the

ALAH ADAMS

plate and saved the day. The nurses, doctors, bloggers, and the ordinary citizens that really care about freedom and the Republic for which it stands! The YouTube channel hosts like Eric Dubay, Truthiracy, Feed Your Mind, Young Pharaoh, Really Graceful, King Heru and countless more that took their time, energy and brilliance to speak truth to power. Always remember that the saga continues, it doesn't end with this victory.

I lost friends because they believed in the hoax to the point that they excommunicated me for going against the mainstream media. I've been ridiculed and ostracized because of my anti-establishment views on this hoax. I was once threatened because someone told me that their relative died from the coronavirus and I should stop promoting the opposite.

It's been an amazing adventure dealing with the Elite1% and this coronavirus hoax. They're already talking about dubbing the coronavirus America's new 9/11. Which was also a planned inside job that they used to take our freedoms with the Patriot Act and Homeland Security Act. The only difference between 9/11 and the coronavirus hoax is that now millions are online sharing truth, when 9/11 happened there wasn't this much of an internet presence.

The Elite1% were able to pull off the hoax of a century, until around 2003–2005 when the internet began to buzz about intel that 9/11 was an inside job orchestrated by the Elite1%, referred to in those times as the Illuminati. The evidence of their involvement was conclusively overwhelming, and millions were able to discern fact from fiction.

Twenty years later, the Elite1% are still at it with this new hoax. They are already posting plans for Agenda 2030, so the next 10 years are going to be very interesting, to say the least. We know that they want to cut the human population in half by 2030, how they plan to do it is a scary question.

All that being said, this is your friendly neighborhood citizen journalist, a/k/a The Millennial Hero Alah Adams signing off.

CHAPTER 15
THE CONCLUSION

YOU ARE THE ONE!

In beginning of this work, I mentioned that I would save a special message for you at the end of this work. I alluded to telling you something at the end, kind of like a special gift for completing this work. Think of it as a mental certificate for finishing a course. The only difference is that this course has made you a conscious soldier ready for the war that has been declared on your soul by the Elite1%. I've said a lot, and I hope that the words were able to uplift and enlighten.

Like I said, in the start of this work, repetition is good! That's something I learned from Gurumayi and the Siddha Yoga teachings. About 33% of my philosophy comes from Siddha Yoga, 33% from ancient teachings, and 33% from life experience with 1% left over for the information learned on the Elite1%.

All of it is a culmination of where I am in the current moment. Circumstances withheld; we are all on the same path to enlightenment. To exist on the physical plane, on this planet, in this time is an amazing experience. The world is quickly becoming conscious on a massive scale! This is an exciting time, because it has the potential to lead us to the utopian society we were meant to be. For the greater good of the whole and not the few. This is the time for a worldwide awakening!

Now let's get to the special information I saved for you! I decided to speak on the Creator as the One. I didn't want anyone to confuse this work with a religious one. I wanted to speak on the Creator, but I didn't want to be partial by referring to Allah, Jesus, God, Jehovah, etc. I wanted this to be about spiritual motivation, not religious rhetoric. So I came up with the concept to call the Supreme Being the One.

It made sense to me for a few reasons. For one, the creator is the One in the essence of what One embodies. The second reason is to teach a simple idea that you're the One, I'm the One, we're all the One! The illusion is that we are all different. You are One of a kind! I could've just told you this empirical knowledge on page one, but it would've defeated the purpose of the travel. We walked through a whole spiritual obstacle course, a virtual spiritual adventure based on the moment and the truth! And we did it together.

Again, give yourself a round of applause and a pat on the back for taking this journey with me. A lot has taken place on this journey, but the most important occurrence was that we have elevated our minds and our spirituality. And for that I want to say thank you for taking this journey with me and stay on the path. I love you dearly, and I really hope that reading this work has assisted you in becoming the remarkable person you were born to be.